HORIZON

MAY, 1959 • *VOLUME I, NUMBER 5*

HORIZON

A Magazine of the Arts

MAY, 1959 • *VOLUME I, NUMBER 5*

PUBLISHER
James Parton

EDITOR
Joseph J. Thorndike, Jr.

MANAGING EDITOR
William Harlan Hale

ASSOCIATE EDITORS
Ralph Backlund
Robert Emmett Ginna

ASSISTANT EDITORS
Hilde Heun
Ada Pesin
Jane Wilson

EDITORIAL ASSISTANTS
Robert C. Agee, Caroline Backlund,
Gertrudis Feliu, Mary Ann Pfeiffer,
Judith Shaw, Martha Thomson

ART DIRECTOR
Irwin Glusker

ADVISORY BOARD
Gilbert Highet, *Chairman*
Frederick Burkhardt   Oliver Jensen
Marshall B. Davidson   Jotham Johnson
Alfred Frankfurter   Richard M. Ketchum
J. H. Plumb

CIRCULATION DIRECTOR
Richard V. Benson

HORIZON is published every two months by
American Horizon, Inc., a subsidiary of American
Heritage Publishing Co., Inc., 551 Fifth Avenue,
New York 17, N. Y.
    Single Copies: $3.95
Annual Subscriptions: $18.00 in the U.S. & Can.
            $19.00 elsewhere

Second-Class postage paid at New York, N. Y.

HORIZON welcomes contributions but can assume
no responsibility for such unsolicited material.

COVER: It is Wednesday. Bahram Gur, the king of Iran, is paying his weekly visit to his Egyptian queen. Gay and pleasure-loving, Bahram Gur married seven princesses of seven countries, built for each a castle of a different color, and visited regularly on different days of the week, clothing himself in the matching color. Bahram Gur was given to vivid imagery: his red Russian queen of Tuesdays was a "honeyed apple, sweet and rosy-hued." To his Roman *aruss* (doll) of Sundays and the yellow castle he said: "The shops close at night; but you, seller of beauty, you must open your shop at night." Bahram Gur lived in the fourth century before Christ. This fragment of a manuscript, dated 1589, is an illustration for the poet Nizami's (1140-1203) *Khamsa*, and is in the Spencer Collection of the New York Public Library. It shows the king and his Wednesday queen seated in a garden pavilion. An article on gardens begins on page 24.

FRONTISPIECE: Glittering with rubies and plumed with pearls, the figures of Saint George and his chalcedonic horse emerge victorious over a writhing green dragon. This twenty-one-inch high reliquary, inset with precious and semiprecious stones, was commissioned by Duke William V of Bavaria, called the Pious, in 1590. It was designed by his court goldsmith, Hans von Schwanenburg of Utrecht, and executed by Hans Schleich of Munich. Within the pedestal, encrusted with a sapphire-and-enamel Bavarian coat of arms, is a drawer containing bones purporting to be from the arm of Saint George. The reliquary is now in the Treasury of the royal palace in Munich.

THE ADVENTUROUS ANGELS

Bold in getting, the Guggenheims have been equally bold in spending on new talents and some mercurial causes

According to legend, on a certain Sabbath eve Meyer Guggenheim, patriarch of the family that was to become so rich and heavy-laden, summoned his seven sons into his study, one by one. To each in turn he showed seven sticks and, one by one, snapped each stick in two. Then, assembling the seven sons, he took up still another seven sticks in a bunch, but try as he would he could not break them. He is said to have told them: "Separate, you are easily broken. Together, none can break you. My sons, be as one."

An air of improbability hangs over this moral tale. In the first place, Meyer Guggenheim was not the sort of man to break forty-nine perfectly good sticks of wood unnecessarily. In the second place, his seven sons were far too shrewd to require such theatrics to teach them the obvious. But whether the legend is true or not, there is no doubt that the very substantial fortune accumulated by the Guggenheims was the result of fraternal teamwork. That fortune grew and grew. At its height, about a generation ago, it was commonly accounted the second largest in America, yielding place only to Rockefeller's long purse. Neither Carnegie nor Vanderbilt was close; and as for Ford, "He is richer than any Guggenheim," ran the quip, "but there are seven Guggenheims."

An acquisitive society celebrates the Acquisitive Man. Whether he be called captain of industry or robber baron, every step on this man's way has its interest: how he got his money, how he got more of it, how cruelly he stamped on whose toes in getting it, why he slowed down in his pursuit

Within the gates of Peggy Guggenheim's Venetian palazzo, this bronze sculpture by the Italian Marino Marini stands facing the Grand Canal. Peggy's treasure palace, which for a decade has been a lively center of the international art world, is now open to the public.

of it, and—in some ways the most fascinating aspect of all— what he did with it. And when, in celebration of the great American fortunes, the question is asked, "What makes the Guggenheim fortune differ from all other fortunes?" there are two chief answers. The first is the speed with which it was put together, and the second is the daring with which it is being spent.

The Guggenheims, father and sons, amassed nearly a quarter of a billion dollars in rather less than fifty years. The money will be longer in the spending, but in the process some of the family have displayed a disposition to take remarkable chances. Of Meyer's sons, the venturesome spenders were Daniel, Solomon, and Simon. Simon's widow has followed her husband in unusual benefactions. Of Meyer's grandchildren, Harry, the present titular head of the family, and Peggy are also highly original patrons. Other Guggenheims have given away large sums of money for one or another estimable purpose; but just these six are responsible for funds and foundations that have already spent or have available to spend something in the neighborhood of $100,000,000, and that have aided a phenomenal array of poets, painters, scientists, and philosophers, helped fledge the wings of American aviation, given to the public in the United States and Italy some excellent collections of modern art, and helped fill American ears with new music. Guggenheim money has provided commissions or support for such varied Americans as Charles A. Lindbergh, Frank Lloyd Wright, Arthur H. Compton, Stephen Vincent Benét, Thomas Wolfe, Aaron Copland, Jackson Pollock, and Isamu Noguchi—all men now renowned in their various fields, though only the first two were widely known when Guggenheim funds came to them. The Guggenheims' fortune came out of the American earth, but in unusually imaginative fashion a few of them have ploughed a great part of it back

By PETER LYON

for the general enrichment.

Meyer Guggenheim came to Philadelphia in 1848, a refugee from a Swiss ghetto. He was twenty years old, he spoke no English, he had no money and no friends, but he was apt, observant, and resourceful. Slowly at first, as a tailor and peddler, then more surely, as manufacturer of stove polish, bluing, and lye and as merchant of spices, he began to build a little pile. It grew with his family. He married in 1852; in the next twenty years his wife presented him with eleven children, eight boys and three girls (one boy died young), and, patriarchally, he sensed that he must provide for his children's future. He invested in the business of making lace and embroidery, and sent three of his sons to Europe to learn about it and to keep a watchful eye on his enterprise. So far Meyer Guggenheim had done nothing that was not careful and sensible. But by 1880 his little pile had grown big enough for him to show that he was truly a Guggenheim, which is to say a mettlesome gambler. He took a plunge into that riskiest of all ventures, silver mining. For $5000 he bought a half interest in two mines, the A.Y. and the Minnie, in Leadville, Colorado.

Like any good gambler, Meyer Guggenheim knew the odds. He knew there had been a gold rush in that neighborhood in 1859-60 and a silver rush in 1877; moreover, the word of bonanzas a-borning was all over the eastern financial community. But when he visited Leadville early in 1881 he must have been discouraged. His mine shafts were flooded; more water gurgled in every hour. Nevertheless, when the other half interest was offered for an additional $50,000, Meyer Guggenheim snapped it up on behalf of himself and a partner. Back in Philadelphia, he learned from a telegram that he had hit the jackpot: "STRUCK RICH ORE IN A.Y. SHAFT NUMBER ONE. YOU HAVE A BONANZA."

For anybody else a property that netted $100,000 a month would have been the clinch, the soft-focus fade-out, the happy ending; but for the Guggenheims it was only a paltry beginning. Mines led to smelters ("The smelters get all the profits," Meyer Guggenheim grumbled; "it's smelter extortion.") and smelters led to more mines. Soon there were Guggenheims industriously scrambling all over the map: one son learning mining in Leadville, another learning smelting in Pueblo, a third buying ore up and down the Rockies, a fourth selling refined metals in the east, a fifth and sixth minding the store in downtown New York, and a seventh sitting down with Porfirio Díaz, the Mexican dictator, to contract for important mining and smelting concessions south of the border. Who could compete with such an energetic and hydra-headed intelligence? "While you're outsmarting six of them," a rival grieved, "the seventh is already two jumps ahead of you."

Meyer Guggenheim's good luck, foresight, and sagacity made millionaires of his seven sons, but they made multimillionaires of themselves. When H. H. Rogers, a guiding genius of Rockefeller's Standard Oil Company, undertook

BENJAMIN   MURRY   ISAAC   MEYER

m. Leonie Bernheim

daughter, Peggy

MURRY AND LEONIE GUGGENHEIM FOUNDATION (*dental clinic, etc.*)

ART OF THIS CENTURY GALLERY, NEW YORK

PALAZZO VENIER DEI LEONI, VENICE

AND HIS SEVEN SONS

DANIEL *SOLOMON R.* *SIMON* *WILLIAM*

Florence Shloss *m. Olga Hirsch*

DANIEL
GUGGENHEIM
FUND
FOR THE
PROMOTION OF
AERONAUTICS
(1926-30)

DANIEL AND
FLORENCE
GUGGENHEIM
FOUNDATION;
son, Harry F.,
President

JOHN SIMON GUGGENHEIM
MEMORIAL FOUNDATION
(*Fellowships*)

MRS. SIMON GUGGENHEIM FUND
(*Museum of Modern Art, N.Y.*)

SOLOMON R. GUGGENHEIM
FOUNDATION (*Museum*)

to set up a smelting trust, the American Smelting and Refining Company, the Guggenheims declined to join, blandly biding their time. At length in leisurely fashion they gathered in the trust designed for their downfall at a profit of some $30,000,000 with themselves in full control of the board of directors.

Their fingers reached out from silver and lead to gold and copper and nitrate; from Colorado and Mexico to Canada and the Yukon, to Chile and the Belgian Congo. When Meyer Guggenheim died in 1905 his sons were worth, according to a student of their assets, some $40,000,000; but they were only fairly launched on their way. Guggenheim steam shovels were scraping the hide off Utah and Nevada and New Mexico in the search for copper porphyries; and investors were gambling on properties with strange names—Kennecott, Nipissing, Esperanza, Santa Rita—on no other surety than the hint that Guggenheims were involved.

The brothers were, however, no longer seven. William, the youngest, grown fretful over what he felt to be arbitrary decisions by his elder brothers, pulled out of the firm and commenced to occupy himself with respectable philanthropies and with such organizations as the Pennsylvania Society and the University of Pennsylvania Club in New York. Then there were six.

Benjamin, the fifth brother, also resigned from the firm and, in 1912, went down on the *Titanic*. Then there were five.

Isaac, the eldest, most colorless, and least effectual brother, died in 1922. Then there were four.

Since these four—Daniel, Murry, Solomon, and Simon in order of seniority—had always been the ablest of the brothers, the disappearance of the others did not weaken the confraternity. Nor did the War of 1914-18 appreciably shave the profits of those concerned with the production of copper. What with one thing and another, it was estimated that by the 1920's the firm of Guggenheim Brothers was worth some $200,000,000.

They had got it; they had got more of it; they had stepped on some toes in their pursuit of it; but now they were slowing down. It was time to reflect on what Francis Bacon had said: "Money is like muck, not good unless spread." One after another, the four brothers established foundations to fork it around.

There is nothing quite so timid as a large sum of money. It might have been expected that the brothers would compliantly follow the course of, say, Carnegie and Rockefeller who, astraddle their moneybags, cautiously and prudently fertilized such fields as education, public libraries, medicine, and public health—each laudable and irreproachable benefactions; each, to lapse into the investor's jargon, a safe, sound two per cent. Indeed, one of the four Guggenheims, Murry, did just that, building and endowing a free dental clinic. But the other three struck out boldly along unexplored paths. They gambled with very risky cards. Two of the bets have paid off, more handsomely than could have been expected; as for the third, there is still some doubt.

First was Daniel. In 1920 he was sixty-four years old and on the edge of retirement from his last directorship. To him came his younger son Harry, a naval aviator in the War of 1914-18 and now bursting with plans to promote aeronautics (it was still a strange and exciting word in 1920). A group of Harry's friends, including F. Trubee Davison and Artemus Gates, were involved. They had impetuously decided that a school of aeronautics had to be founded, and Harry, then thirty years old, had undertaken to draft a letter to be circulated amongst one or two dozen men who might be counted on to finance what was, at the time, a bizarre and ticklish enterprise. Young Harry's one condition on accepting this responsibility was that it be understood he would send his letter to no member of his own family. But he did want to make sure the letter was properly phrased, and so he showed it to his father.

He had written a better letter than he had thought. His father read the draft and at length looked up. "I want to do this myself," he said. In this way the Daniel Guggenheim Fund for the Promotion of Aeronautics was formed, and before long its founder was digging a ceremonial spadeful of dirt at New York University's School of Aeronautics, for which a wind tunnel and propeller laboratory were to be built along with classrooms for three professors. "As I am an old man," said Dan Guggenheim, "I shall dedicate the rest of my life . . . to aviation . . . the greatest road to opportunity which lies before the science and commerce of the civilized countries of the earth today."

The Fund, created at a time when there was little popular interest in aviation, built a Full Flight Laboratory at

"*The Guggenheims will be awfully sore at me if I don't get down to writing pretty soon.*"

Mitchel Field where for the first time an aviator (the then Lieutenant Jimmy Doolittle) took off, flew, and landed while guided solely by instruments. It provided an equipment loan that enabled operation of the first regularly scheduled commercial airline in the country. With its aid, the first weather-reporting service was organized for the benefit of passenger airlines, and six schools of aeronautical engineering were established. The Fund also sponsored Charles A. Lindbergh after his historic solo flight across the Atlantic in 1927, promoting and paying for a nation-wide tour in his *Spirit of St. Louis* that gave to Americans by the millions a personal glimpse of adventure in the skies.

By 1930 aviation was no longer a chancy enterprise, and the Fund, having accomplished its purpose at an expenditure of $3,000,000, was terminated. Yet its president, Harry Guggenheim, continued to promote pioneering ventures through the Daniel and Florence Guggenheim Foundation. While experts snickered, financing was extended to the remarkably prescient Dr. Robert Goddard for his rocket research. (When in May 1940, Guggenheim arranged an appointment for Goddard to offer his research and developments to ordnance specialists, an army officer remarked, "Very interesting, but we don't think rockets will play any part in this war; this war is going to be fought with the trench mortar.") Guggenheim money also paid for Jet Propulsion Centers at Princeton and Caltech (1949), an Aviation Safety Center at Cornell (1950), an Institute of Flight Structures at Columbia (1954), and a Center for Aviation Health and Safety at Harvard (1957).

Here is a sufficiently notable record but in a limited field and one in which, by summoning a little hindsight, it is possible to say that any shrewd philanthropist could have done the same. But when Simon Guggenheim, in turn, undertook to spend *his* money, he took all knowledge and all art for his province and did so, it still seems today, daringly.

In 1925 he launched what he named the John Simon Guggenheim Memorial Foundation in honor of a son who died at seventeen just as he was about to enter college. He had been a boy of intellectual promise; that had vaguely suggested to his parents a fund that would (as it was subsequently phrased in the charter) "promote the advancement and diffusion of knowledge and understanding, and the appreciation of beauty. . . ." A praiseworthy aim, but how to achieve it? The family turned to Carroll Wilson, a former Rhodes scholar, who had become general counsel of American Smelting and Refining, and he in turn sought out Henry Allen Moe, then a youngster fresh from his own Rhodes scholarship. Wilson metaphorically gave Moe a blank sheet of paper, bidding him return it when it was filled out with the best possible plan for spending Simon Guggenheim's money. The result was the Guggenheim Fellowships, awarded annually to scholars, scientists, and artists, with no strings attached.

As a program it was and is unique in conception. Fellows

chosen by juries of experts in their fields were to be given money for whatever they wanted to do—including, if such was their whim, doing little or nothing. Even now, thirty-four years later, the scheme seems to offer unlimited possibilities for folly. Give money, perhaps, to a seasoned and sensible scientist for some sort of practical experimental work, preferably hitched to a sound commercial manufacturing enterprise; but throw it away on some buffleheaded youngster who plans only to paint a picture or write a poem or, worst of all, just go abroad and moon through European galleries and spend Guggenheim's good American dollars in European cafés?

Yet this is what was soberly intended, and what was actually done. In retrospect it is difficult to praise too highly the wisdom with which the Foundation's work was planned and has been administered. In 1925 there were fifteen Guggenheim Fellows who were given some $2000 apiece. As the Foundation has grown—its assets are now worth more than $45,000,000—the value of the dollar has decreased so that today the Fellows (three hundred in number last year) get grants up to a peak of $7500. They need never even report what they have done with the money.

At first even some of the Foundation's advisers had their misgivings; the secretary general, Henry Allen Moe, was urged that there were some fields of endeavor that would not lend themselves to Fellowship support. Poetry, for instance. "If you give a poet money so that he can write poetry," Moe was told, "nothing will happen." Take 1926, the second year of the Foundation's existence, and glance over some of the projects on which good money was spent:

A study of the quantum theory of the nature of radiation.

The topology of the interior of the atom and the structure of molecules, with especial reference to the nature of the chemical bond.

Spectral series relations in extreme ultraviolet metallic spectra.

Researches on Bohr's almost periodic functions, on haphazard motion, on periodogram analysis, and other topics.

Creative writing in poetry.

Moreover, the grants in these subjects were all made to men not yet famed in their own specialized fields and in any case very little known outside of them. In order:

Arthur H. Compton, a subsequent Nobel Prize winner who was to become one of the scientists most intimately concerned with atomic fission.

Linus Pauling, later to win the same prize in chemistry.

Ralph Sawyer, subsequently Dean of the Graduate School of the University of Michigan, whose Fellowship work on the spectrographic analysis of metals was to become of material aid to our country in wartime.

Norbert Wiener, presently professor of mathematics at M.I.T., and a guiding spirit in the science of cybernetics.

Stephen Vincent Benét. "When he applied for the Guggenheim Fellowship in December, 1925," his wife wrote

"*Frankly, Miss Ellis, the Guggenheim Foundation had been led to expect a book of poems.*"
DRAWING BY GARDNER REA; © 1937 THE NEW YORKER MAGAZINE, INC.

later, "he was twenty-seven years old. He had a wife and a child under two. Another child was to be born in early fall. He lived entirely by his writing and he wanted very much to take time to write a long poem. To say the Fellowship meant a great deal to us under those particular circumstances is to deal in understatement. It was, in this case, exactly the reverse of Dr. Johnson's bitter definition of a patron: 'One who looks with unconcern on a man struggling for life in the water, and, when he has reached ground, encumbers him with help. . . .'"

That Fellowship resulted in *John Brown's Body.*

Once Benét had delivered the manuscript of his poem to his publishers, he went off on a holiday. He returned to find his book was selling in a fashion unprecedented for a poem; it had been selected by the Book-of-the-Month Club; presently it would be awarded the Pulitzer Prize. Understandably delighted, he hastened to the Foundation's offices to thank his benefactors and their secretary, Henry Allen Moe. "Let's not be silly," Moe told him. "It is *I* who must thank *you*. Hereafter, if anyone objects to granting a Fellowship to a poet, I have only to point to you."

And if the selections made in 1926 seem exceptionally fortunate ones in the retrospect of 1959, by 1999 it may have developed that the true movers and shakers from amongst the Guggenheim Fellowships were chosen in some quite different years, and for quite different reasons. But there can be no doubt that the Foundation has proved itself an unexampled investment in American futures. Four Nobel Prizes—to Hermann Muller in physiology and to the late James Sumner in chemistry as well as to Compton and Pauling—and twenty-nine Pulitzer Prizes for creative writing and musical composition testify to the ability of those who have, over the years, selected the Guggenheim Fellows

9

in those fields; and the roster of Fellows in the fine arts is like a roll call of all that is liveliest and most vigorous in American artistic creativity.

Have the Foundation's selection committees ever erred by rejecting a candidate who later turned out to be first-rate? Certainly—just as they have erred by picking some candidates who turned out to be duds. Plainly, the selection will always involve some risk. Simon Guggenheim was himself aware how speculative the work of his Foundation would be. "He used to say," Moe has recalled, " 'When you are grubstaking, you take chances. You act on the best evidence you've got, but still you've got to take chances, because nothing is certain in the end.' And that," Moe concluded with some satisfaction, "is the way we have always tried to operate."

"One gambler per family is enough," Mrs. Simon Guggenheim seemed to say when she set about her own program as patron of the arts quite apart from the Foundation. Indeed she has tried to narrow the odds with uncharacteristic caution for a Guggenheim even by marriage. Twenty years ago she began to donate paintings and sculpture to the permanent collection of New York's Museum of Modern Art; they number, thus far, forty-four. "Mrs. Guggenheim expressed the wish that the museum use her funds to acquire works of the highest excellence," Alfred H. Barr, Jr., director of the museum's collections has said. "Only such works, she felt, would have permanent value and were, therefore, indispensable to the museum." In short, the museum was to buy, if possible, only "sure" things. It is a sumptuous collection that has thus been built up over the two decades, including eight Picassos, five Matisses, four Légers, a Braque, a Chagall, a Gauguin, a Hopper, a Miró, two Modiglianis, Rousseau's *Sleeping Gypsy*, and sculpture by Brancusi, Maillol, and Rodin. It also includes Peter Blume's *The Eternal City*, which as it happened was conceived and in large part painted while Blume was on a Guggenheim Fellowship.

Nor is Mrs. Guggenheim an absentee donor, all money and no further interest. The museum, of course, makes the selections; but that she has an influence on them is widely understood. Any day of the week may see her arriving at the entrance door unexpectedly and unannounced, to roam through galleries on reflective inspection tours.

But, as the seasons rolled, what of the other Guggenheim brothers? Murry, we have seen, had endowed a dental clinic; Isaac and Benjamin were dead; William, a singular fellow who contributed to the presidential campaign of Alfred M. Landon by presenting him with a bust of Benjamin Franklin, at length produced a curious autobiography in which he fondly appraised himself, in the third person, as a "creative cosmopolitan club-man . . . orthodox only when he happens to agree with popular sentiment." There remained only Solomon.

It was left to Solomon to undertake the most incautious and aberrant of possible benefactions, the espousal of ex-treme avant-garde art.

Whence this unlikely passion? Solomon had for years enjoyed the reputation of being the fun-loving Guggenheim; was this an elaborate jape to spoof respectable art lovers? Actually, it was quite seriously intentioned. Before the First World War he had peered curiously into the unfamiliar world of the art dealer and expert, the world where he feared that any murky portrait by an early Dutchman might be attributed to Rembrandt and any cinquecento painting to Titian. With more confidence he had bought some American landscapes and some examples of the Barbizon school. Growing bolder, about 1930 he began, under the enthusiastic tutelage of the Baroness Hilla Rebay, to buy the work of such abstract painters as Kandinsky, Delaunay, Gleizes, Léger, and Mondrian; since the Baroness excessively admired the work of her countryman Rudolf Bauer, he also bought some dozens of that German artist's paintings. By 1937 he had endowed his own Museum of Non-Objective Art—with the Baroness as its director—in which his collection was displayed, usually at knee-level. In these odd surroundings the Baroness was in her element. "You must be very careful," she urged a young painter who applied for a museum scholarship (not to be confused with a John Simon Guggenheim Fellowship), "in not modulating with light and dark if you want to express cosmic rhythm and create the feeling of elevating spirituality."

Bemused critics wandered through these exhibitions, listening to the music by Bach that issued from concealed loudspeakers, referring now and again to the dense prose in the catalogues (written chiefly by the Baroness) and wandered out again, still wondering. "Spectres," murmured the critic for *Art News*. "A religious cult set to incidental music," said the eminent Edward Alden Jewell of *The New York Times*. But what Solomon had done in fact was to get in on the ground floor, or perhaps even the bargain basement, of the vogue for abstract art that was to prove so overwhelmingly popular in the 1950's.

Meantime, in London, Solomon's niece Peggy, a daughter of Benjamin Guggenheim, had likewise interested herself in avant-garde artists and their art. A generous and impulsive woman, she had been gliding for some years through their Bohemian atmosphere as patron, close friend, and hostess at spectacular parties. In 1937 she decided to open a gallery in London. Like her uncles before her, she was shrewd enough to seek out able advisers. The painter Marcel Duchamp helped make her gallery—named Guggenheim Jeune—a lively success in every way except the financial one. Then, when she concluded that she would rather lose money on a museum of her own than on a gallery, she engaged the critic Herbert Read to be museum director.

The proximity of another Guggenheim in the sacred groves of non-objective art seemed to vex the Baroness Rebay. She dispatched a peppery note to Guggenheim

Jeune, sputtering with Teutonic syntax: "Due to the foresight of an important man since many years collecting and protecting real art, through my work and experience, the name of Guggenheim became known for great art and it is very poor taste indeed to make use of it, of our work and fame, to cheapen it to a profit."

But Peggy Guggenheim was undaunted. When the second war interfered with her plans for a museum in London, she descended upon Paris where, with the help of a list prepared for her by Herbert Read, she launched on a whirlwind buying campaign, coming away with a kind of *smörgåsbord* of all the chief trends in modern art from 1910 to 1940. After various alarums and excursions she arrived in New York, complete with her collection and the surrealist painter Max Ernst, who was briefly to be her second husband. She went around to pay her respects to her Uncle Solomon's museum. "It really was a joke," she wrote later. At the Hotel Plaza, where the Solomon Guggenheims maintained a huge suite and a collection of their own, she visited her Aunt Irene, sitting amongst Picassos, Seurats, Braques, Klees, Kandinskys, and Chagalls. Peggy Guggenheim, a forthright niece, urged her to burn all the Bauers in Uncle Solomon's museum and move these treasures there instead. "Shush!" said her aunt. "Don't let your uncle hear that. He has invested a fortune in Bauer."

By October 1942, Peggy Guggenheim was ready to open in New York a new gallery, Art of This Century, surely the most eccentric pleasure dome ever decreed for the inspection of art. Lights flashed on and off, with great rushes of sound pulsing rhythmically, walls were concave, paintings swung in mid-air from strings, and the critics reeled as though on a storm-tossed ocean liner.

As it happened, her appearance could not have been more perfectly timed from the standpoint of the painters who comprised America's own avant-garde. It was as though they had rubbed the magic ring, and lo! here was their fairy godmother. For the group that was to become known as the Abstract Expressionists, Peggy Guggenheim's outrageous gallery was a home away from home. Jackson Pollock, Mark Rothko, Adolph Gottlieb, Robert Motherwell, William Baziotes, Ad Reinhardt, Jimmy Ernst, Richard Pousette-Dart, Clyfford Still—one by one she tendered them their first one-man shows.

With the end of the war Peggy Guggenheim removed once again to Europe, this time to her Palazzo Venier dei Leoni in Venice. If her Uncle Solomon had been miffed by the way she had upstaged him in the field of abstract art, he gave no sign. In any event, he had a surprise of his own up his sleeve: a new museum to house his collection, and to be designed by Frank Lloyd Wright. The commission held interest, in part because Wright's views both on modern art (It is "crime without passion") and on museums ("What is the museum but a kind of morgue?") had some currency. Never a man to be cowed by an inconsistency,

Wright drew the plans for the celebrated hollow cylinder of concrete that now crouches beside New York's upper Fifth Avenue. Wright reported that tears stood in Solomon Guggenheim's eyes when he first looked at the design. "Mr. Wright, this is *it!*" he exclaimed. "I knew you would do it." The museum was completed this spring, the most recent specimen of Guggenheim beneficence.

They are a glittering company, all these various gifts the Guggenheims have thrust upon us. There no longer seems to be much of a future for the six-million-dollar Daniel and Florence Guggenheim Foundation in the world of space, since the government in Washington is annually doling out billions for space research and hardware. Harry Guggenheim may still pull a few rabbits from his sleeve. He is by now also the president of his Uncle Solomon's Foundation, in which capacity, eight years ago, he and the trustees replaced the Baroness Rebay with James Johnson Sweeney as director of the Museum of Non-Objective Art. Not long afterward its name was changed to The Solomon R. Guggenheim Museum. Much of Rudolf Bauer's *œuvre* was demoted to the storeroom and the Klees and Picassos and Chagalls resurrected. Quality by selection, Sweeney announced, not quantity by collection, would be his ruling principle; and New Yorkers began to look forward to a visit to the new museum to see how it might differ from the Museum of Modern Art. At all events, the latter museum will continue to be enriched by the acquisitions made possible by Mrs. Simon Guggenheim; and one way or another, one can be reconciled to the fact that Peggy Guggenheim has decided to house *her* two-million-dollar collection permanently in Venice. And if, after a surfeit of abstract art, visitors to the Guggenheim galleries feel as though they have been munching glass, they can reflect upon the annual largesse of the John Simon Guggenheim Memorial Foundation, bringing the fruits of knowledge and creativity in not one but a dozen fields.

"*Exegi monumentum aere perennius,*" sang Horace—"I have built me a monument more enduring than bronze"—and a careful ear can detect a sardonic note of self-ridicule. For while Horace may have hoped that his lines would lilt along the centuries, he also knew he sang them thanks to the patronage of a certain rich man called Maecenas. The patron is remembered today only because he supported Horace and Virgil and a few other poets.

Before too very long the fact that some men named Guggenheim gouged a fortune out of the earth may also be forgotten. But it seems likely that they will, after all, also be remembered for their patronage; it will be more enduring than their copper and lead, even than their silver and gold.

Peter Lyon, a free-lance writer, contributed "When Man First Left the Earth" to the first issue of Horizon *and collaborated with C. W. Ceram on "The Blue Museum" in the second.*

Picasso's Night Fishing at Antibes, *bought by Mrs. Guggenheim for the Museum of Modern Art*

Henri Rousseau's The Sleeping Gypsy—*a 1939 donation*

Left, another gift: Picasso's Girl Before a Mirror

Mrs. Simon Guggenheim

I. MRS. SIMON'S FUND

Less unconventional in her ways and means of philanthropy than other members of the family whose ventures are illustrated on the following pages, Mrs. Simon Guggenheim is nevertheless the donor of a list of phenomenal works by major modern masters. First aroused to an interest in contemporary art by the historic New York Armory show of 1913, Mrs. Guggenheim bided her time until the Museum of Modern Art was founded and then, in 1938, inaugurated a fund to help the museum enrich its collections with examples chosen with an eye to their having "permanent value." In her own home, she has been the collector also of early Renaissance painters such as Crivelli and Filippino Lippi. But to the Modern Museum she has given, along with a long list of other key works, no less than eight Picassos—including the *Girl Before a Mirror* shown below, opposite ("simultaneously clothed, nude and X-rayed") which still puzzles some visitors. She is also a trustee of the museum and sits on the committee that passes on acquisitions—sometimes works produced on John Simon Guggenheim Fellowships.

Maillol's The River *reclines in the Modern Museum's garden*

The Russian Expressionist Vasily Kandinsky's Black Lines, No. 189 *(above) painted in 1913, along with Modigliani's* Nude *of 1917 (below) and Brancusi's* Sorceress, 1916 *(right), exemplify the museum's continuing interest in insurgents.*

14

II. UNCLE SOLOMON'S MUSEUM

One of the most startling structures ever designed by Frank Lloyd Wright—and the only example of his work in New York City—was completed this year to house Solomon Guggenheim's own showplace of avant-garde art on Fifth Avenue (below). Founded in 1937 as an educational institution dedicated chiefly to non-objective and abstract work, it now houses the world's largest collection of Kandinsky (180 pictures) and America's largest museum group (170) of Paul Klee. It supports contemporary artists by buying work fresh from studios and through its biennial International Award. Last year's winner of the $10,000 prize was the Spaniard Joan Miró. Some New Yorkers, astonished by Wright's building, whose galleries run on a continuous spiralling ramp, have likened it to "a concrete ice cream cone" or "a silo for art."

Solomon R. Guggenheim

HERMANN J. MULLER
1932—Physiology

SCIENCES

ELMER D. MERRILL
1951—Botany

JAMES B. SUMNER
1937—Chemistry

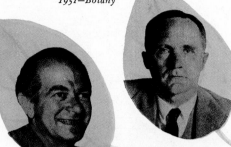

LINUS PAULING
1926—Chemistry

WILLARD FRANK LIBBY
1941—Chemistry

HARVEY E. WHITE
1941—Physics

JAMES A. VAN ALLEN
1946—Physics

NORBERT WIENER
1926—Mathematics

ARTHUR H. COMPTON
1926—Physics

AARON COPLAND
1925—Musical Composition

THE ARTS

VLADIMIR NABOKOV
1943—Creative Writing

ANTONIO FRASCONI
1952—Graphic Arts

STEPHEN VINCENT BENET
1926—Poetry

ROBERT PENN WARREN
1939—Creative Writing

GIAN-CARLO MENOTTI
1946—Musical Composition

PETER BLUME
1932—Painting

Secretary General Henry Allen Moe (right) tends the hardy plant of the John Simon Guggenheim Memorial Foundation, which under his care since 1925 has awarded Fellowships to nearly 3,500 artists, scholars, and scientists. Above is a sampling of well-known Americans who have received grants in various fields—in some cases (as the dates show) when only beginning upon their careers. The Foundation has also supported Canadians and Latin Americans.

THOMAS WOLFE
1930—Creative Writing

JACK LEVINE
1945—Painting

ISAMU NOGUCHI
1927—Sculpture

JOHN KENNETH GALBRAITH
1955—Economics

LIONEL CASSON
1952—Classics

ELIZABETH STEVENSON
1951—American Literature

ALFRED KAZIN
1940—Literary Criticism

BERTRAM D. WOLFE
1949—European History

PAUL H. DOUGLAS
1930—Economics

DOUGLAS SOUTHALL FREEMAN
1952—American History

EDMUND WILSON
1935—Literary Criticism

HUMANITIES

LOUIS B. WRIGHT
1928—English Literature

III. A FAR-REACHING FOUNDATION

A white eighteenth-century Venetian palace, rich in gardens, houses the collection that Peggy Guggenheim (a niece and rival of Solomon) has been building since 1938.

Miss Guggenheim's surrealist paintings include the one below by her former husband Max Ernst. Her collection also embraces numerous cubist, dada, and abstract works.

The dark-haired owner of the Palazzo Venier dei Leoni peers out from behind a wood sculpture.

IV.
PEGGY'S
PALACE

A colorful heiress and volatile mover and shaker in the art world, Peggy Guggenheim ran her own avant-garde gallery in New York before transferring operations to Venice. In 1951 she opened her collection along the Grand Canal to the public, and since that time it has been one of that city's sights. Young Italian artists receive her munificence as young Americans did before them. Two years ago, dashing the hopes of American museum directors who would gladly have housed still another Guggenheim collection, she set up a fresh foundation of her own and in effect bequeathed her personal storehouse of striking works to a pleased yet astonished Venice.

THE FUTURE
AMERICAN CLASS SYSTEM

Old concepts of "upper" and "lower" will give way before sweeping

realignments of talents and status, says a young man in politics

Practical politicians, concerned with today's divisions and tomorrow's votes, do not usually sit down to write essays on the broad future of their society and their own role in it. But Stimson Bullitt, a Seattle attorney who has held municipal and county posts, served on numerous campaign committees, and run twice for Congress on the Democratic ticket, is an unusual politician. As a guide for aspiring practitioners, he has written a short book of medium and long-range observations entitled To Be a Politician *(Doubleday & Co. 1959). Its final chapter, from which this article is taken, contains some challenging thoughts on coming changes in this country's social and cultural makeup.*

Throughout this country's history the chief boundary between our political parties has been changing. Sometimes it has been regional. From 1930 to 1950 the primary fault line separating them was between haves and have-nots. Since then it has been hard to find. A political fortune awaits the first able politician to locate the next 50-yard line. It may be on the complexities which we have made for ourselves: perhaps imaginative versus unimaginative, educated versus uneducated, boldness versus caution, conformity versus noncomformity, closed versus open mind. Or the difference may depend upon the window through which one sees the world.

The new main division may be between a liberal upper class and a conservative lower one. For in America, the economic class system is disappearing. Although it cannot yet be said that redistribution of wealth and income is compressing to a pancake the cone of economic ranks, the combination of the raised floor and the truncation of the tip has ended economic inequality's political significance. At the same time, a new class system on the basis of socially desired talent is being created by the removal of the barriers of race and birth. A person can now rise or fall faster and farther than before. The old observation about "shirt sleeves to shirt sleeves in three generations" will be contracted to one, and then will cease to be true because each person can wear the same clothes as anyone else.

Our numerical proportion of talented people has not changed, but they used to be scattered through society. Now that persons are allowed to rise or fall to a level which their talents fit, they are developing, through association, a sense of community or class with those whose talents are the same. The growing trend of gifts, either direct or through foundations, from businesses to colleges is an example of the new link between some of the talented people in each, as well as of the recognition by business executives that men and women with advanced schooling are needed to manage our economy. The degree of such association, creating a sense of class, is increased as family ties are loosened by many causes, one being the free choice of companions made possible by technology and social equality. People are tending to have companions more like themselves than are most of their own kin. A recent example is that of Harlow Curtice and his brother, both employed by the General Motors Corporation, one as president and the other as a machinist. They had little to do with each other, although it is said that their mutual feelings were cordial. In the past such brothers probably would have been engaged in similar work, would have had closely overlapping circles of friends, and would often have eaten at the same table.

Another cause tending to stratify into a class those on the same level of talent is the awareness of each person that everyone who knows him recognizes that he belongs where he is, while formerly judgment on him was reserved because his ability was not proved by his rank. When impediments have been removed from each person's rise or fall to the level which his ability fits, either he will have no excuse for his low station or he will deserve full credit for his high one. This condition may make people feel more comfortable with others on their own level. Its stratifying force may be stronger upon those on the lower levels, who may feel anxiety and depression at the knowledge that they belong

By STIMSON BULLITT

where they are and that this fact is known by all who know them. In the past most individuals felt a reservation about scorning those below because they knew that but for the grace of the social system their positions might be reversed. Coming discomfort between persons on different levels will be mitigated by two things: first, recognition that the background factors which determine status have been shifted from social setting to personality, from outer to inner gifts, and second, the greater understanding that now exists between classes. In the past the members of the ruling classes, from Marcus Aurelius to slave traders, hardly regarded members of the laboring classes as human beings. And poor folk used to regard some of the nobility as embodiments of more marvelous qualities than they possessed in fact. To some extent the serf would live vicariously, through the lord of the manor, some aspects of life such as adornment, grace, valor, and the regular eating of meat.

Accurate sifting of abilities will divide society into haves and have-nots of talent rather than wealth. Instead of a sharp division between upper and lower there will be a scale of imperceptible grades from Newton to Jukes.

The shape of society when classified on the basis of talent will resemble not an hourglass but a fishing bob, or a pair of coolie hats laid brim to brim, with a spike projecting from the apex of each. More of the people will be clustered near the equator which divides the two classes. However, the spread between the two extremes of talent—the spikes at the top and bottom—will be greater than in the past. Those on the south spike, on the level of legal incompetence, will be unable to benefit by opportunity and comfort, and so will remain as low as ever. Those on the north spike will have greater advantages than the most privileged aristocracy of the past: fewer hours of mechanical routine, a higher level of education, and, most important of all, the challenge of first-rate company undiluted by well-born dolts and drones.

However, these extremes will be so small in proportion to the mass in the middle that in politics they will not matter much. The middle will have enough wealth and skill of collective action to take care of the south pole and enough competent leaders, for most things, to be independent of the north. After all, politicians will make up a small proportion of those on the upper spike, most of whose occupants will be seminal minds which make new worlds, while politics is more concerned with judgments that make the present world go round.

With the abolition of inherited titles and all but minimal inherited wealth, the members of the new upper class of talent will not, without a radical reversion to the old ways, be able to pass their status on to their children except by an upbringing that assists them to develop their talents and to wish to use them. Nor can these members keep their status for themselves except by their own continued efforts. They will have no vested interest in things as they are except the right to have their talent recognized. Unlike wealth, whether inherited or acquired by effort, talent can neither be given nor taken away by social change. Most of the bolder and more imaginative members of society will be among the upper class, and they will be more favorable to experiment and less disposed to resist change than the lower class, which will have lost its more daring members to the upper class.

Those who remain in the lower class or who descend to it will compose a group more stagnant and limited in its thinking than the old working class, which had the leavening of the more able men who used to be a part of it. Labor unions now find it difficult to obtain leaders among the younger men. The appeal of class loyalty has gone; so has the goad of class hate. The success and peace of the labor movement have dampened the idealism of all but a few incorrigible zealots. The most gifted of the youth in working-class families have left for more rewarding work which has been put within their reach by the removal of hereditary bars. If they have the ability, those who want money go into business or medicine; those who want security join the armed forces, become schoolteachers, or get civil service jobs; those who want fame go into entertainment, politics, or sports; those who want idleness, freedom from responsibility, or time for leisure pursuits work for a big company at short hours; those who want power can get more for the same price in fields other than labor.

The blurred boundaries between horizontal grades will make it easier for each person in the middle ranks to ignore his exact status or to misrepresent it to himself. Social mobility may increase anxiety but reduce discontent. Lower-class resentment against the upper may be stirred by little

The class system common to most societies of the past resembled a low pyramid (left), with the aristocratic few at the top and the more numerous poor and unprivileged at the bottom. Since ability was generally irrelevant to one's place in it, the talented people (red figures) were scattered throughout the structure. But when talent becomes the determining factor, as Mr. Bullitt foresees (at right), the gifted will rise to the top, displacing the merely rich or wellborn. Society will then assume a bulbous shape: the most able will be at the very peak, the great bulk of the population will cluster in the middle, and the incompetent will drop to the bottom.

except a person's knowledge that despite the presence of a marshal's baton in his knapsack he remains a private. If strong frustrations should develop in the lower class and not be relieved by the leadership, it seems probable that there would be a temporary period of violence by the lower class and conservatism by the upper. Except for such aberrations, however, these new conditions will tend to make the upper class liberal and the lower class conservative.

Another cause pushing the lower class toward conservatism in its politics is that it is becoming the more leisured class. Unlike wealth, work is not becoming more evenly shared. The patterns of our technology are changing in a direction that reduces the proportion of unskilled work to skilled work. In relation to skilled persons, fewer unskilled men are necessary to build a rocket ship than a steam ship. The probable result is shorter hours for unskilled jobs than for skilled jobs. By reason of each class's opportunity and choice, the lower class will work less than the upper. As in ages past, the idle rich will be supported by others, but now by the more able rich instead of by slaves.

With enough abundance, the comparative economic worth of talents becomes less important as a factor in setting work hours than the personal cost of work to the individual. In terms of a person's attitude toward his own time, interesting or pleasant work costs less than dull or disagreeable work. Four hours on a garbage truck are the equivalent of a longer period at a desk in a bank. When everyone has plenty of money a reduction of hours is a more effective improvement in a person's employment conditions than is a raise in pay. Already some jobs are preferred for the satisfaction or pleasure of their performance despite a lower rate of pay than is available at other jobs. And the elements of competition and joy in work, the incentives for longer hours, are largely confined to skilled work.

With less time at work than the upper class, the lower class would spend more time at play. Always in the past, members of the laboring class were uncultivated in the arts of leisure, and when their time came for play they were tired. But when members of the lower class can start to play when they wake up in the morning, tired by nothing but yesterday's play, and when they have had a chance to cultivate the arts of leisure, they may engage in more active amusements than were practiced by the former laboring class. Already they have begun. In this respect their choice of amusements may be like the dancing, hunting, and conversation practiced by the small leisure classes of the past.

Politics will continue to be a vocation of strenuous work. In some vocations a rise in average pay will cut the work load by attracting more persons into the field. But in politics, where much of the work cannot be done well unless concentrated in a comparatively few hands, an increase in pay may only intensify the competition and induce politicians to work harder than ever.

In some vocations an imposed limitation of hours would protect practitioners from being beaten out by the more industrious, and therefore would encourage compliance with the rules. But in politics limitations on hours, whether agreed, decreed, or legislated, would be unenforceable if tried and against the public interest if successful.

The device of sabbatical years, however, might alleviate the comparatively harsh terms of labor in politics. While it is not practical to blow a whistle, making politicians quit work three hours after lunch, each politician for a full year during the middle of his term could be prohibited, on penalty of forfeiting his office, from appearing at any scene where public policy is formed or set in motion. Such absences would not appreciably impair his capacity to perform in office and in some ways would improve it. Instead of merely throwing the rascals out, we may in the future throw out the good ones too, at regular intervals, inviting them to have a rest and then come back.

The accuracy of placement under the new class pattern will tend to identify as such those persons who combine intelligence and honesty in the highest degree. Their leadership in opinion formation will be greater than it has been in recent years, when most people have had enough knowledge with which to form a basis for an opinion and yet have been uncertain as to who were the real experts. These accurately labeled masters in their field may come to lead opinion to a greater extent than has been done by anyone since the days when ignorance forced most people to form their opinions on subjects beyond their experience by relying on some leading members of the ruling class.

Intellectuals may be expected to shift their political allegiance from the underprivileged poor, who will disappear *as a class*, to the able, most of whom will have above-average incomes, or whatever will have become the measure of success.

Substantially more than half of the Jews may be expected to be found in the upper class. It is ironic that not until now could the Jews be thought a superior people, whether chosen by God or by chance. In antiquity their contribution to civilization, though substantial, was not comparable to that of the Greeks and Romans; between then and the recent past they lived in isolation and obscurity with modest accomplishments for a time in Spain, later in Turkey, Holland, and elsewhere. But the exclusion of non-Christians from landownership forced Jews to live in the towns and thereby become adapted to urban culture. This head start gave a cumulative advantage to their descendants. Perhaps an even stronger factor is that urban life under persecution made them the only recognizable group in the world that has been subject to the process of natural selection on the basis of brains for a period of enough generations for it to take effect. At the same time, they retained their straight and narrow outlook longer, emerging late from their form of Middle Ages, and now are in a delayed renaissance. Thus, in most of those areas of endeavor which we think important there is, and for a while in America there will continue to be, soaring achievement, not of Judaism but by Jews.

This new class system already has collided with the American tradition of a politician's identification with the community which elects him. The top grades of talent have become concentrated in urban centers of thought, renown, and wealth, while Congressmen still are elected according to population on an even geographic spread. Lord Bryce observed this condition in *The American Commonwealth* before the turn of the century, and ever since it has grown less necessary and more acute.

The dissolution of roots in the community of one's birth has refined and accelerated the sifting process. Because the talented have migrated to the metropolitan centers in a higher proportion than the untalented, the merit of the average officeholder in relation to the importance of the office is lower in the United States House of Representatives than in any other public employment, possibly excepting some police forces.

By custom, though not by law, well-established residence in the district still is a condition of election to the House, even though the conflicts of geographic interest have relaxed. A local cluster of communities no longer preserves in isolation a distinctive nature calling for loyalty and understanding which can come only from a deep attachment. The rise in the rate at which persons shift their homes is reducing the time period required to establish enough local identity to qualify for Congress. However, the wait still is substantial in all districts and longest in those long-settled, half-deserted areas where the supply of talent is most short.

Every state has urban centers which, in a lesser degree, stand in relation to the rest of the state as Paris has stood to the rest of France. The Senate does not have to take a crop from many barren zones. But many Congressional districts have no large town and no college that deserves the name. In such districts young men and women worth their salt depart when done with school, returning only for visits of sentimental condescension. Those left behind are persons tending to lack education and imagination, indifferent to the world and how it works. One of them, perhaps the best, goes to Congress to shake the earth. In most of these districts voters receive little choice. The country stands to gain if more young persons equipped for national problems take the gamble of settling in the provinces. If they do not, either the residential requirement will be removed, as in England, or the authority of the House will drop.

Unlike the way of political life when both upper and lower classes produced leaders, under the new system political leaders will come only from the upper class. They may be born of parents in the lower class, or of one parent in each, but before they become leaders their talents will have identified them with the upper class. Formerly, men of working-class parents could attain this identification only after the achievement of leadership, if ever.

These leaders of the new lower class will try to climb even higher in the upper class by promoting the interests of the lower. They will choose to become leaders of the lower class for two motives: preference for the conservative philosophy, and the wish for a position of leadership in a field where the number of such positions in both classes is limited and of about equal desirability in each.

When everyone lives on the same levels of comfort and opportunity there will be no more leaders from deprived beginnings and no more voters awed by the comparative majesty of their leaders' station. Among leaders of the same rank there no longer will be a wide range in the length and steepness of their climb. For voters living in comfort, aware that the leaders are not much better off than they, there is less need to live through some splendid figure of a leader. So perhaps people will choose leaders who are more like than superior to themselves, who are of the upper class but not far up. After the 1920 election Wilson Mizner remarked that he had not realized until then the truth of his mother's reminder to him as a child that anyone can be elected president. Now maybe both aspects of this double meaning will become the common custom.

The policy issues between the parties formed by these two classes will not be comparative comforts or rights to take part in government; they will be the manner of approach to all problems, perhaps an opposition of liberal versus conservative—as distinguished from the present secondary division of sentimental humanitarianism versus decayed liberalism and a vision of the old days looking splendid in the dusk with the light behind them. It may be that more than half of the liberal leaders will be found in policy making positions in the executive branch, which has become the main originating source of policy, while a greater proportion of conservative leaders may go into the legislative branch, which in its now reversed position primarily vetoes, approves, adjusts, and corrects.

Whatever the basis of division between the parties in the future, it is certain only that the line will not be between dumb and smart, or bad and good, with all wisdom or virtue on one side. This approach has been the ground for separation in the eyes of narrow partisans. As upon the extinction of the Federalist and Whig Parties, followed promptly by a Democratic Party split, a patent concentration of merit does not last because it attracts the whole electorate, and so the process of division into two disputing parts has to start again.

GARDENS SINCE EDEN

They have given delight to people of every age and land

By NAN FAIRBROTHER

We have no idea what the Garden of Eden looked like. There are pictures of course in plenty—it has been a favorite subject for painters—but even if we suppose they knew any more of the matter than we do, they do not help us. For gardeners may be interested in gardening, but painters are interested in painting, and the pictures they like to paint are seldom of gardens but more often of pretty young women without any clothes.

So it is Eve they show us, not Eden. The garden, for painters, we cannot help suspecting, is no more than a flattering green background for Eve's white nakedness. It is no use our peering curiously into odd corners of the picture to see what this first of all gardens was really like.

Certainly there are spaces of canvas left over from the serious business of painting Eve's charming head and most seductive bare feet, but the spaces are never filled with helpful vignettes of designs for laying out gardens. And even if they were, the gardens would not be Eden but only the gardens the painters happened to know—medieval castle gardens, or gardens like Persian carpets, or later on imposing layouts in the manner of Versailles. But in any case nothing in the least to do with first beginnings.

"God Almighty first planted a Garden," so Francis Bacon opens his famous essay, and there we must leave Eden and pass swiftly over the mythical, gardenless history from the Fall to the Flood, for as another gardening writer

EGYPTIAN TOMB PAINTING *A Pond in a Garden* AT THEBES (ABOUT 1400 B.C.)

very cautiously says: "The Advances Gard'ning made from Adam's Expulsion to the General Deluge, is dubious, there being little left of it."

What we do know is that man from the start has delighted in gardens. In many early European languages the same word *paradise* is the name for both heaven and garden. Paradise is a garden, and men of all persuasions have agreed with Thomas Traherne that

All Bliss
Consists on this
To do as Adam did.

The first gardens we know about as fact, not flowery fancy, are the gardens of Egypt and China, and these two quite different types have continued to the present day as two different kinds of gardening: the Egyptian as the formal style; the Chinese as the natural landscape garden.

European civilization began in the Eastern Mediterranean in Sumer and Egypt and spread round the shores of this inland sea. Since the Mediterranean lies on the edge of the great desert belt of the northern hemisphere, the climate is hot and arid and the natural vegetation sparse and dried out by the summer heat. So that what men long for in their gardens is coolness and shade, somewhere moist and luxuriantly leafy to escape to "when the fierce heat dries up the moisture in the mouth and the scorching wind consumes the very marrow of the bones."

25

But if trees and flowers are to thrive in such a climate they need help. They must be sheltered from scorching winds, and from marauding animals (including man), and above all they must be constantly watered. So in these gardens there is always water for the cool relief of men and plants alike: water lying in pools, falling in fountains, flowing in channels to irrigate the blossoming trees and flowers. And this need of shelter and water has dictated the style of Mediterranean gardens from the start, has meant that despite the changes of history and art, the early gardens are all of the same family and only the details vary. Since they must be rigidly enclosed, they are small. Since they must be irrigated, the ground plan is formal. And since the world outside the walls is hot and dry and desert, the gardens are as thrivingly green and leafy as water and gardening skill can make them.

Living in our moist temperate climates where all the land is a natural wild garden, it needs an effort of understanding to realize how luxurious these small flowery enclosures must seem in the lands where they belong, how a flourishing green plant is a cherished delight, like a deep drink to the spiritually thirsty. We can feel it faintly in the paintings from Egypt and Rome, and in the constant Eastern pictures of gardens of flowers set in leaves, treasures as precious and as delightful to the senses as jewels against velvet.

This then is the underlying pattern, the small enclosure of flowering plants which we recognize at the start in the tomb painting from upper Egypt (*preceding page*): a lotus pool surrounded by close-planted trees and shrubs and enclosed in a rectangular wall. Egyptian gardens, like many early gardens, were often religious. They were attached to temples, and the trees and flowers, although they were no doubt first chosen for their beauty, were given religious significance as well, as the rose and lily were later on in the monastery gardens of Europe. In Egypt the lotus was the flower of the dead and various trees were held sacred to the gods. The fig tree was highly valued and tame monkeys were trained to gather the fruit into baskets.

These gardens of Egypt were loved and copied by her successive conquerors, and they spread to Syria and Rome and Persia and India as the empires of the Mediterranean rose and fell. For all men are friends in their gardens, and once inside the garden gate the question of who is conqueror or conquered ceases to matter. Gardeners are more concerned with exchanging favorite flowers than with quarrels.

So the Egyptian garden was copied everywhere, and though there are local variations in the different lands and climates, we recognize with pleasure always the same enclosed oasis of fragrant leafy shade, a fragile paradise more enduring than all the empires because it is constantly created afresh by man's unchanging delight in trees and flowers in an arid climate.

It is the same garden traced out lovingly in the Persian carpets, the same in the Roman frescoes, and if the Hanging Gardens of Babylon (*page 28*) look more like a classical temple than a garden, that is only because the picture was drawn by a Western artist intrigued by the ingenious architecture of his imagined construction. For as the ancient writers describe them, the Gardens of Babylon were very different. They were built perhaps for the half-mythical Semiramis or else (for the legends vary) to please a wife from the mountains of Persia who sighed for the hillside gardens of home. The terraces were planted with flowers and shrubs which were watered from the nearby Euphrates, and the supporting pillars were hollow and filled with soil so that tall shade trees could root and grow. The accounts disagree over details, but quite certainly the gardens were not laid out in Renaissance-style beds as the artist here so confidently shows them.

The pleasure gardens of Rome were a growth of the peaceful Empire and were a chief charm of Roman villa life. The style came from the East and they are variations of the gardens we know already, less tyrannously controlled by the milder climate of Italy. Water is still used, but the plan is less rigid, and the high walls dwindle in

this peaceful setting. The villas at Pompeii (besides the more notorious decorations) are delightful with frescoes of painted gardens. The one from Rome (*below*) is very similar: a garden room in the villa of the Empress Livia. It was built underground to escape the summer heat, and the walls were painted in an unbroken fresco of trees and flowers and singing birds. Not that all Roman gardens were in such charming taste, for as we might guess the Romans had a mistaken fondness for topiary, and Pliny had a horrible habit of spelling out moral maxims in clipped box edging.

But the true style is still of gardens which are roofless rooms for outdoor living, a style which continues unbroken through European history—in the cloister gardens of the Dark Ages, the courtyard gardens of Moorish Spain, and (*page 30*) the castle gardens of the Middle Ages. And the style spread East through Persia and Afghanistan to India, for Babur, the Mogul conqueror, was also the "Prince of Gardeners" and loved the little regular gardens of Persia, taking the formal style with him on his Eastern conquests to India where the Moguls laid out elaborate gardens as settings for their tombs. Babur himself was buried in a garden of Judas trees.

In the three thousand years from the Egyptian lotus pool to the medieval pleasance there is no great change in these little gardens which people loved and lived in, sat in, and slept in, little enclosures separate and complete in themselves as a room is. They were seldom planned with the house and were often at a distance, carefully walled-in against enemies with a locked door for entrance. As history became less violent the walls were lowered, the garden spread a little and was laid out with more formality. But the great change in European gardens came with the Renaissance, that sudden astonishing growth of man's spirit which carried him forward into the daylight of intellectual confidence. He is no longer satisfied with the little shut-in plots that have comforted him through all the dark centuries of his history till now. He feels himself suddenly magnificent. And from these modest enclosures of flowers he makes gardens which are magnificent too. For Renaissance gardens are no longer mere homes for plants, they are works of art, architectural constructions that use vegetation as their building material. The plants have no longer any personal-

FREDERICK DURAN-*Rome of the Caesars*, PHAIDON PRESS

A ROMAN GARDEN: FRESCO FROM THE EMPRESS LIVIA'S VILLA. THE TREES INCLUDE A POMEGRANATE (LEFT), OAK (CENTER), AND QUINCE (RIGHT). BETWEEN THE OAK AND THE BIRD CAGE GROW POPPIES. THE WHITE FLOWERS NEAR THE BIRD CAGE ARE POPPIES. THE PINK FLOWERS, ROSES.

THE HANGING GARDENS OF BABYLON: A RENAISSANCE ARTIST'S CONCEPTION

ity of their own; they are there to fill the places allotted to them in the design. Trees and shrubs are not valued for their beauty but because they will stand constant clipping, and flowers are chosen for their neat and disciplined growth. They are none of them there for their own green sakes but as malleable material for man's own self-expression.

Renaissance gardening is one of the fine arts, and best considered not as gardening at all but as a form of stately ceremonial music, a superb overture to the palaces it surrounds and the princely life for which it is the background. The gardens are not designed by gardeners but by architects, sculptors, painters—by the great names of the Renaissance—and Le Nôtre himself was trained as an architect before he turned to gardens for his material.

For the gardens which were created in Italy and France in the late sixteenth, seventeenth, and eighteenth centuries are no longer simple, detached enclosures without relation to the house they serve. Renaissance man was confident with a new sense that he controlled his world as a whole, was triumphantly master of his environment. So garden and house are laid out together, doors and windows open freely onto courtyards and terraces, and these continue into the garden by noble staircases and open walks and long vistas.

But this superb control was not learnt all at once. In his essay "On Gardens," Francis Bacon makes the following observation: "A man shall ever see that when ages grow to civility and elegancy, men come to build stately sooner than to garden finely." In the early Renaissance we can see

how true is Bacon's judgment. The new style of palaces is already well developed while the gardens which surround them are still no more than a series of the little enclosed plots we know already, numbers of them merely laid out side by side till the ground is covered "like the honest bachelor's feast, which consisted of nothing but a multiplication of his own dinner, three legs of mutton and turneps, three roasted geese, and three buttered apple pies."

But these are nonetheless Renaissance gardens. The bricks they are built with may be old-fashioned, but the conception is new. The garden is not yet controlled as the unified whole which Le Nôtre will create later on in France, but already there are avenues, vistas, a progression from one part to the next, and above all the house merges with its setting.

Like the rest of the arts the Renaissance garden first blossomed around Florence, but Rome soon followed the new fashion and the Italian princes outdid each other in laying out splendid pleasure grounds. The popes and cardinals especially were most ambitious planners in this grandiloquent new style.

Partly from necessity but more from choice, most Italian gardens were laid out on hills. It follows therefore that terraces and flights of steps had to play a large part in the design, and these architectural elements of gardening the Italians learnt to handle superbly well. They were also blessed with a wealth of fine statues, both antique and modern, and these were set everywhere on pedestals about the gardens. The fall of the land they skillfully made use of to construct elaborate waterworks: cascades and fountains and flowing waterways of the greatest ingenuity. They had, too, a disarmingly childish taste for watery practical jokes, for innocent-looking benches that drenched whoever sat on them, and fountains that suddenly shot water over unwary passers-by. It is odd to think of the stately Renaissance nobles giggling and screaming in these elaborate settings.

Most famous of all for its water was the villa of Tivoli near Rome, where a river is diverted down the steep hillside gardens through a maze of water fancies. Montaigne was most impressed by it in the sixteenth century, and so was I in the twentieth. I think the garden can never have been more enthusiastically wet than when I went there once in a flooding thunderstorm. Renaissance water was tamed in pipes and kept in its place, but there was nothing tame about the river and the rain which poured down together through Tivoli when I was there. All the steps were turned to waterfalls, all the terraces to lakes, and every tree to a natural showering fountain. There was no way of knowing which was Renaissance water engineering and which was modern rain. The whole world was drowned and washed away in torrents.

In these vast pleasure grounds there was generally a smaller *giardino secreto*, a secret garden somewhere near the house. Not that it was a secret at all by our standards, being simply another formal enclosure with statues and fountains, but still an enclosure kept for the use of the family, a private place as the rest of the grounds quite certainly were not, being full of courtiers and visitors and often of the public as well. For Renaissance gardens presupposed an audience. They were displays to impress the Joneses. It is only that these Renaissance Joneses were princes of such truly civilized taste that the gardens which impressed them were quite genuinely magnificent.

Yet it was not in Italy that the Renaissance garden reached its perfection. Fine as they are, these gardens are also faintly theatrical. Walking round them from one brilliantly contrived prospect to the next, we are reminded again and again what wonderful back cloths they make for the stage. There is some further possible experience, we feel, which they never quite achieve. And when we see what the Renaissance garden becomes in France under the genius of Le Nôtre we realize what it is.

Unlike the Italian gardens, Le Nôtre's designs are a single indivisible unit. He can control the whole of his immense material at once in a way no Italian gardener achieved. He does not build up his plan by adding pieces together but conceives the entire garden as a setting for the house, fusing the two together into a single work of art. The palace controls the vistas and the axes of the garden; the garden controls the setting and proportions of the palace. (Indeed at Versailles the gardens were laid out before the final palace was designed.) The two belong inevitably together, like a head to the body.

Since Renaissance palaces were symmetrical, Le Nôtre's gardens are symmetrical too, at least in the parts we can see in any single prospect. They are mostly on level or deliberately leveled ground and laid out on a long central axis which carries the view unhindered from the house to the far distance. Le Nôtre composed with three main elements: the levels of ground and water, the upright walls of trees and hedges, and the open space of the sky. With these he created a new ideal landscape, decorating it sparingly with fountains and statues, using the different textures of mirrorlike pools and clipped hedges and in more distant parts of the grounds the feathery tops of freely growing trees. His best gardens are of an austere and classical perfection; our mind travels nobly over level spaces, down long canals of quiet water, through avenues of stately trees, and on into the world beyond. The gardens of Le Nôtre convince us with a godlike sense of order and serenity. These are the gardens of man's intelligence; and the pleasures of intelligence, so Poussin said, are above all others.

But we may not always feel up to Poussin's standard. Even the Renaissance French were not always so intellectually strenuous, and if this noble symmetry was not what they happened to feel like, then there were all kinds of frivolous gardens for their amusement, hidden in the trees which filled the spaces between the main vistas of the grounds. There were mazes and topiary and elaborate games with fountains, flowers, and trees in tubs (Le Nôtre loved orange trees). There were grottoes and little pavilions and open-air theaters with walls of green hedges. At Versailles Louis XIV held his court fetes out-of-doors in the gardens: parades and masques and fireworks and elaborate ceremonies, where Lully composed the music and Molière wrote plays for the theaters in the *bosquets*. And it seems always incongruous to think of Molière's powerful, even savage, comedies in this elaborately artificial setting of courtly pastimes.

Le Nôtre laid out many noble gardens which soon became world-famous. Versailles in particular was envied by every prince in Europe. And in the century and more that followed, these royal gardens were copied all over the civilized world. Sometimes the results were worthy of the models, as in Austria and Russia, but sometimes they were much less happy, like the European gardens in China which look very odd indeed and quite irresistibly like fairgrounds.

Versailles is the apotheosis of the formal garden, but what of the others—the landscape gardens which we know of first from the paintings of ancient China? The landscape style, though really no more natural than the formal garden, gives the impression that this delightful scene we have come on is simply a happy accident of nature. There is no question here of a plot enclosed, nothing formal or symmetrical, no straight lines or rigid divisions; the trees and shrubs seem to grow by chance, as if without human interference.

It is a style which needs great skill and sensitivity if it is

Ar intencion de
parler des iar
dins et de lart
de leur talonitai
te et de toutes les herbes qui
y sont semees pour nourris

selon lordre del a b c selon
le latin et en diray la berti
qui puet aidier et nuire
au corps. Car ce bault
especial a ceulx qui demeu
rent aux champs qui ne

to succeed, and it needs a fertile climate if the plants are to thrive without irrigation. The artistic Chinese made landscape gardens of great beauty, as did the Japanese in the same tradition, both full-scale landscapes and miniature gardens which were copies of favorite scenes. In Japanese gardens symbolism is all-important, and rocks in particular have special meanings and traditional positions. Gardens have many values for the Japanese besides the visual pleasure in the scene before them. Yet they love flowers with passion, handling their various beauties with the greatest sympathy, keeping special festivals to admire the blossoming of the cherries and other favorite flowers.

In India the Moguls used the landscape style to lay out parks for recreation, and Marco Polo in the thirteenth century came back from Peking with admiring descriptions of the pleasure grounds of the Kublai Khan. But no one believed him, for whether they lacked the skill, or the climate, or only the taste to appreciate such subtle and unemphatic beauties—for whatever reasons—Western gardeners had no conception at all of a landscape style. What interest there was in ornamental planting outside the enclosed garden had been concerned with trees—trees for temples and sacred groves, worshiped as shrines or dedicated to the gods.

Many peoples from earliest times have felt that trees were sacred, and the Middle East has held them in particular regard. The warlike Xerxes once fell in love with a beautiful plane tree, winding its branches with gold chains and bracelets, setting a guard to watch over it, sending it messages as if to his beloved. It is the one thing I can always remember about Xerxes, and I never open a children's alphabet book without hoping to read that "X is for Xerxes, the king who loved a tree."

But the love of trees and of landscape had little influence on European gardens till the eighteenth century. It was then in England that the romantic landscape style developed in revolt against the tyranny of formal gardening, and it quickly grew to the height of extravagant fashion. Its most famous exponent was Lancelot Brown, nicknamed Capability Brown because he would always find "capabilities" of improvement in the sites he was given for gardens. He designed in a deceptively simple-seeming style with sweeps of grass and clumps of trees and picturesquely winding water, using this natural material to emphasize the inherent character of the landscape.

The ground is not leveled but left with hills and hollows, the water lies unconfined in spreading pools and natural rivers, and the boundary is invisible, screened by belts of trees or a fence sunk out of sight in a ditch called a ha-ha (because visitors, coming on it by surprise, were wont to exclaim "A-ha!"), so that we are not conscious of any distinction between the park and the countryside beyond. For the effect to be aimed at is of nature enhanced by art, but by art which is most carefully hidden.

In nineteenth-century Europe there was no significant new garden style. The formal garden continued or was revived, though the classical vision was lost, and by the end of the century the herbaceous border and the woodland garden developed in revolt against the mechanical degeneration of carpet-bedding. As for our own twentieth century, we have been so overwhelmed by the wealth of new plants which pour in from all ends of the earth, that we scarcely have time to consider the design of the garden at all, but only how we can successfully grow all these new treasures.

But nonetheless there are signs that we are evolving a new garden style to suit our new age, and, in America especially, gardens are being created which are as clearly modern as the architecture they are designed for. Since twentieth-century gardeners have neither the space nor the labor to cultivate a large area, these new gardens are small, often no larger than the ground plan of a house, or even of a single room. And more than any European gardens before, they are part of the buildings to which they belong. Formal gardens were designed as a setting for the palaces they surrounded. Spanish patios were roofless extensions of the domestic dwelling space. But the best of these new American gardens form with the house a single indivisible organic unit: house and garden merge into each other like the fingers of clasped hands. The walls of rooms are continued into the garden, the floor surface is the same inside and out, only an invisible film of glass separates the roofed space of the house from the open space of the garden. As in Japan, the boundary is not between house and garden, but between the house-garden unit of living space and the outside world.

It is a new kind of garden in the West, a creation of twentieth-century America, and I can only agree with the words of the Reverend William Hanbury in 1758, when he said "I may perhaps be reckoned an Enthusiast when I assert that I am really surprised that Men of Fortune do not employ their Time in this manner. I am very certain that the other Amusements they run into are so far from being able to stand in Competition with that more profitable one (of gardening) that the very naming of them with it would be sufficient Invective: Let each Gentleman consider them in his own Mind: He will see the force of what I say: Let him reflect upon Horses and Dogs, Wine and Women, Cards and Folly etc., and then upon Planting. Will not the last engross his *Whole* Mind, and appear worthy of employing all his Attention? Can there be a more genteel, a more rational Amusement? Can any thing tend more to the preserving of Health, and the prolonging of Life? Can any thing be more innocent, or productive of greater Pleasure?"

Nan Fairbrother wrote her first book about country life, An English Year, *while her husband was serving in the R.A.F. and she was living on a farm in Buckinghamshire. Her second book was* Men and Gardens. *Miss Fairbrother cultivates her garden in London.*

On following pages: GARDENS SINCE THE RENAISSANCE

DOMENICO FONTANA

The Renaissance Garden

ANDRE LE NOTRE

The symbolic figure of a Renaissance gardener, shown on the facing page with his tools, is revealing. With one exception, his implements are not tools for making plants grow, as we might expect in a gardener, but for stopping them growing. Shears and scythes and billhooks, hoes and rakes and saws— these are weapons to fight and subdue all free vegetation. Only the watering can is there for encouragement, and that is only to comfort the trees and flowers already most thoroughly tamed and imprisoned in pots.

The proud and wealthy men who laid out the gardens shown on the following eight pages wanted grounds to match their villas. The earliest of these showy gardens are multiple versions of the small, enclosed gardens of earlier days. Such was the garden of the Villa Medici in Rome, built about 1560 and shown in plan in the second of the following two-page engravings. The mount on the right in this plan was a curious feature much used in the gardens of northern Europe; it was a little artificial hill climbed by a winding path and may have had links with the sacred mounds of the Middle East and the Hanging Gardens of Babylon.

By the beginning of the seventeeth century, the energetic jockeying of the papal princes for power and position had put an end to the simple gardener, and the garden designer was in full sway. Domenico Fontana was the first of a family of garden architects who landscaped the villas of the papal princes at Rome and Frascati. His garden for the Roman villa of Cardinal Paolo Savelli Peretti appears in the first of the following two-page engravings.

The garden designers of France were slow to follow the Italian style. They clung to their moats and to turreted walls, and they had a special fondness for the decorative beds known as *parterres de broderie*, elaborate flowing designs picked out with low hedges, generally of box—box, "patient of the scissors." These parterres were usually filled with colored sands, not flowers; flowers were a slight vulgarity in the Renaissance garden. This style—often executed by versatile embroiderers who worked the same designs in fabric for the clothes of the French court—was very popular in France, though it did not suit the more austere taste of the great garden designer André Le Nôtre: only fit for nursemaids, he said, to admire from the nursery windows.

Le Nôtre, the climactic figure in the long development of the formal Renaissance garden, was assigned by Louis XIV to design the palace grounds of Versailles. While he pursued his grand designs with a free hand, he was flanked by a staff of expert assistants whose task it was to execute ingenious grottoes, mazes, labyrinths, green theaters, and spacious pavilions for open-air meals. The canal which adjoined the Basin of Apollo (the third of the two-page engravings) was the largest garden canal ever built and was used by the King for his mock naval battles. The demand for new fountains taxed the ingenuity of the engineers. In addition to such handsome creations as Apollo rising from the lagoon, there were fountains which balanced balls on their jets, played music, or threw off colored water. There were fountains in the form of trees with water raining from their branches, series of overhead fountains which never wet strollers underneath, and hidden fountains which did. ("Decidedly it was an ignoble form of humor," grumbled Henry James of such devices two centuries later.)

Fountain designers went out from France to all the courts of Europe. Men like François de Cuvilliés, who was "Counsellor and Architect of His Imperial Majesty" in the court at Munich made bizarre extensions of the French style, like the fountain on page 40. Europe was overrun with French gardeners, but none of their creations matched that of Le Nôtre, who made of Versailles one masterful synthesis of all the formal garden art which had gone before.

Beginning on the facing page:

A PORTFOLIO OF FRENCH AND ITALIAN GARDENS FROM CONTEMPORARY ENGRAVINGS

Habit de Jardinier,

A Paris, Chez N de L'Armessin, Rüe St Jacqs, à la Pôme d'or,   Auec, Priuil. du Roy

VEDVTA DEL GIARDINO DELL' EMINT.^{MO} SIG. CARDINALE

1. Aspetto del Palazzetto felice.　　2. Giardini secreti.　　*Architettura del*

Giō. Battā Falda del et inc:

OVERLEAF: *The view from Louis XIV's apartment at Versailles. In the foreground is the Basin of Apollo, with the god in his chariot pulled by four horses, and behind it the artificial lake where the King staged mock naval battles.*

COURTESY WEYHE GALLERY

LO SAVELLI PERETTI VERSO SANTA MARIA MAGGIORE

l.ᵉ *Domenico Fontana*. 3. *Teatro e fontane auanti il Palazzo felice.* 4. *Fontane de leoni.*

G. Iac. Rossi le stampa in Roma alla pace con Priu' del S. Pont.

VIEW OF THE GARDEN OF THE MOST EMINENT SIGNOR CARDINAL PAOLO SAVELLI PERETTI LOOKING TOWARD SANTA MARIA MAGGIORE"

Domenico Fontana's design includes a "secret garden" (2), outdoor theater and fountains (3), and two lion fountains (4).

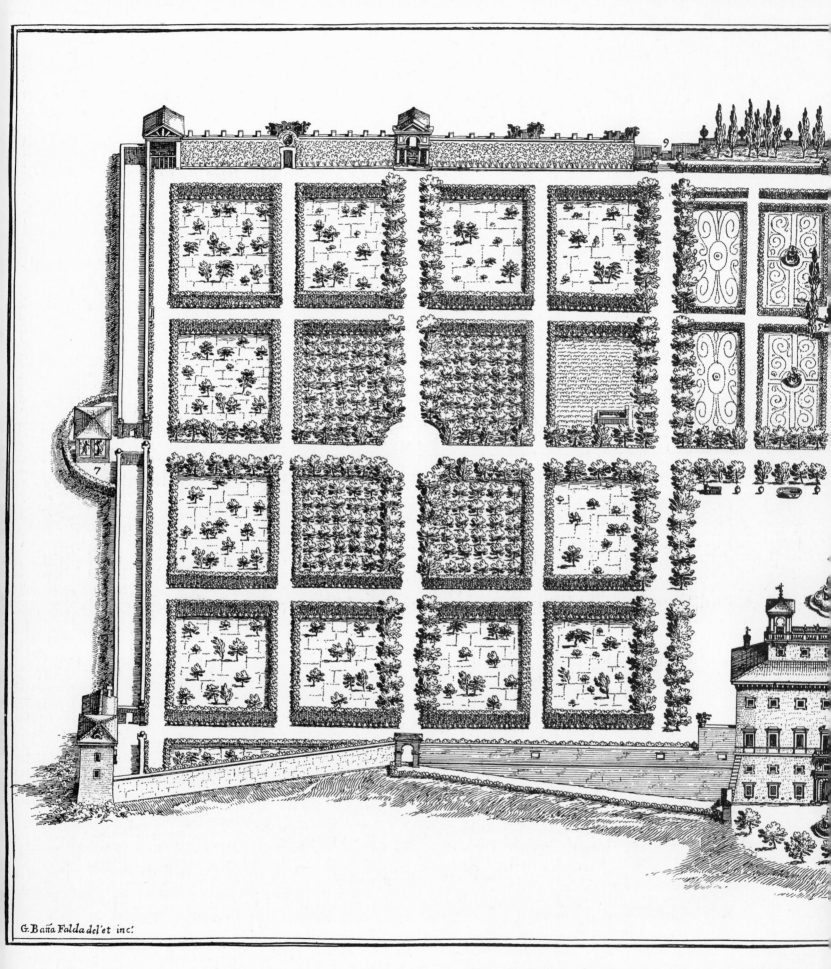

G. Baña Falda del'et inc:

"PLAN OF THE GARDEN OF THE MOST SERENE GRAND DUKE C

Annibale Lippi's design includes a sculpture gallery (3), obelisk with hieroglyphs (5), mausoleu

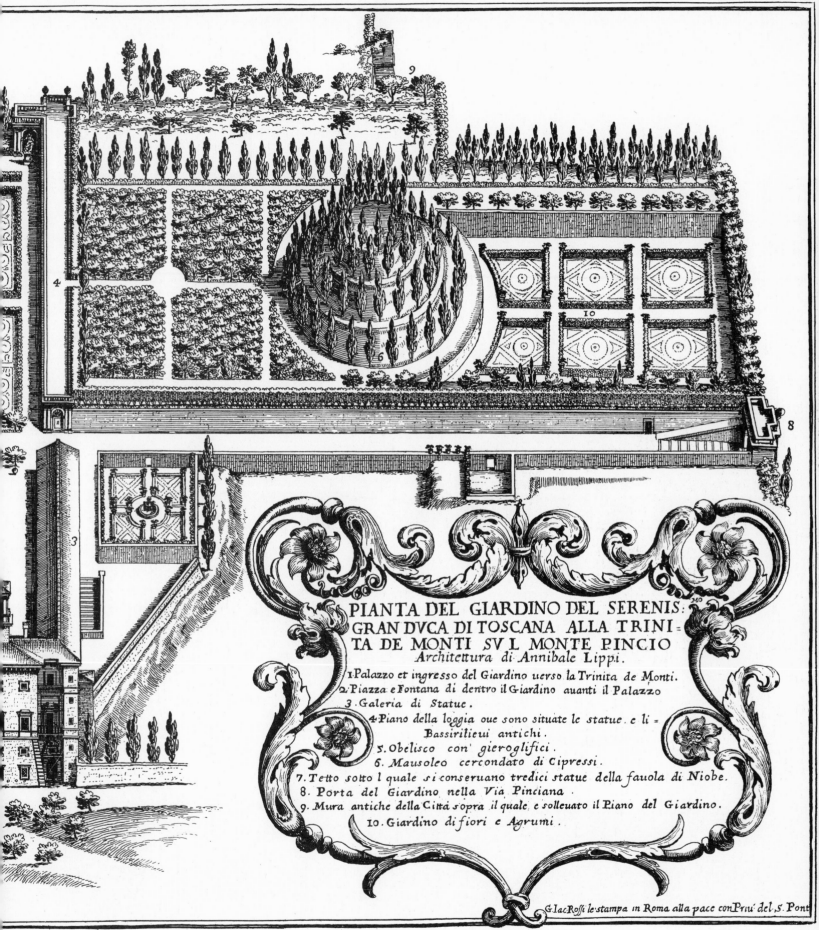

PIANTA DEL GIARDINO DEL SERENIS:
GRAN DVCA DI TOSCANA ALLA TRINI=
TA DE MONTI SVL MONTE PINCIO
Architettura di Annibale Lippi.

1. Palazzo et ingresso del Giardino uerso la Trinita de Monti.
2. Piazza e Fontana di dentro il Giardino auanti il Palazzo
3. Galeria di Statue.
4. Piano della loggia oue sono situate le statue. e li = Bassirilieui antichi.
5. Obelisco con' gieroglifici.
6. Mausoleo cercondato di Cipressi.
7. Tetto sotto l quale si conseruano tredici statue della fauola di Niobe.
8. Porta del Giardino nella Via Pinciana.
9. Mura antiche della Citta sopra il quale e solleuato il Piano del Giardino.
10. Giardino di fiori e Agrumi.

G. Iac Rossi le stampa in Roma alla pace con Priu del S. Pont

USCANY LOOKING TOWARD TRINITA DE MONTI ON MONTE PINCIO"

rounded by cypresses (6), roof under which were kept thirteen statues of the legend of Nairobi (7).

LE B'ASSIN D'APOLLON *est Scitué audessous de l'allée Royalle qui regarde l'appartemen* *char de Triomphe tiré par 4. cheuaux de metail. à ses costez sont les sigures des 4. vents. qui soufflant à* *Piece d'eau ou Canal de 750. thoises de long, sur 40. de large, et 7. pieds de profondeur la Croisée qui ue*

Perelle fecit

oy. sa figure est octogone de 36. pieds de large et dans son milieu Appollon est representé dans son
ioües dans leurs conques iettent en mesme tems l'eau de tous costez. sur la mesme ligne on decouure la grande
Menagerie à Trianon à 450. thoises de longueur.

a Paris Chez N. Langlois ruë s.t Iacque à la Victoire. Auec priuilege du Roy.

Design for a baroque fountain at Munich

THOUGHTS ON GARDENING

If you would be happy for a week, take a wife: if you would be happy for a month, kill your pig: but if you would be happy all your life, plant a garden.

CHINESE SAYING

Imagine that you have ridden in summer for four days across a plain; that you have then come to a barrier of snow-mountains and ridden up the pass; that from the top of the pass you have seen a second plain, with a second barrier of mountains in the distance, a hundred miles away; that you know that beyond these mountains lies yet another plain, and another, and another; and that for days, even weeks, you must ride, with no shade, and the sun overhead, and nothing but the bleached bones of dead animals strewing the track. Then when you come to trees and running water, you will call it a garden. It will not be flowers and their garishness that your eyes crave for, but a green cavern full of shadow, and pools where goldfish dart, and the sound of little streams. That is the meaning of a garden in Persia.

Passenger To Teheran BY V. SACKVILLE-WEST

There is no ancient gentlemen but gardeners, ditchers, and grave-makers; they hold up Adam's profession.

Hamlet, ACT V, SC. I

And forth, withoute wordis mo,
In at the wiket went I thro,
That Ydelnesse hadde opened me,
Into that gardyn fair to see.
And whan I was inne, iwys,
Myn herte was ful glad of this,
For wel wende I ful sikerly
Have been in paradys erthly,
So fair it was that, trusteth wel,
It semede a place espirituel.
For certys, as at my devys,
Ther is no place in paradys
So good inne for to dwelle or be
As in that gardyn, thoughte me.
For ther was many a bridd syngyng,
Throughout the yerd al thringyng;
In many places were nyghtyngales,
Alpes, fynches, and wodewales,
That in her swete song deliten
In thilke places as they habiten.

FROM The Romaunt of the Rose;
TRANSLATED BY GEOFFREY CHAUCER

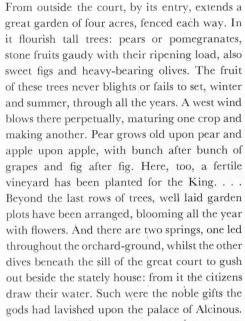

From outside the court, by its entry, extends a great garden of four acres, fenced each way. In it flourish tall trees: pears or pomegranates, stone fruits gaudy with their ripening load, also sweet figs and heavy-bearing olives. The fruit of these trees never blights or fails to set, winter and summer, through all the years. A west wind blows there perpetually, maturing one crop and making another. Pear grows old upon pear and apple upon apple, with bunch after bunch of grapes and fig after fig. Here, too, a fertile vineyard has been planted for the King. . . . Beyond the last rows of trees, well laid garden plots have been arranged, blooming all the year with flowers. And there are two springs, one led throughout the orchard-ground, whilst the other dives beneath the sill of the great court to gush out beside the stately house: from it the citizens draw their water. Such were the noble gifts the gods had lavished upon the palace of Alcinous.

The Odyssey, BOOK VII, DESCRIBING THE
GARDEN OF ALCINOUS, KING OF ITHACA

RECIPE FOR COWSLIP CREAM

Take the Cowslips when they are green and in Blossom, and bruise them in a mortar, and to a good handful or two so done put a quart of Cream and boil it up gently with them. Put in a blade of Mace, season with fine sugar and Orange-Flower water. Strain it and draw it up with the yolks of two or three Eggs, and clip off the tops of a handful of the Flowers and draw up with it and dish as you please.

The Art of Cookery
BY JOSEPH COOPER (COOK TO CHARLES I OF ENGLAND)

The tulipomania was at its height between the years 1634 and 1637, but some time before this the enthusiasm of Dutch amateurs had already forced the prices of rare bulbs up to a ridiculous figure. . . . For one 'Viceroy' bulb, paid for in kind, the following goods were given: 2 loads of wheat; 4 loads of rye; 4 fat oxen; 8 fat pigs; 12 fat sheep; 2 hogsheads of wine; 4 barrels of 8-florin beer; 2 barrels of butter; 1,000 lb. of cheese; a complete bed; a suit of clothes and a silver beaker—the whole valued at 2,500 florins. One bulb of 'Semper Augustus' fetched nearly twice that sum, together with a fine new carriage and pair.

Tulipomania BY WILFRID BLUNT

GARDEN OF THE CASTELLO DI MONTALTO PAVESE IN ITALY'S PO VALLEY (EIGHTEENTH CENTURY)

Inside a hedge of yew, the garden contains clipped bushes of box, beds of geraniums, begonias, ageratums, and coleus.

AN EIGHTEENTH-CENTU
PERSIAN GARDEN RUG

Persia: Flowers and Water

The Persians so loved their flowery gardens that, when they traveled or were driven indoors by winter weather, they carried with them elaborate colored rugs which were picture plans of the cherished gardens they had left. These rugs were wall hangings rather than floor coverings, and this one shows a pool with four channels flowing out between beds of trees and flowers. One of the most famous was the Winter Carpet of King Chosroes in the sixth century. It was sixty yards square and showed a garden in spring. The soil was gold thread, the water sewn with crystals, and the flowers and trees embroidered with precious stones.

The Mogul conqueror Babur the Tiger was also an enthusiastic gardener, and as he traveled about on his most unpeaceful missions he peacefully collected the flowers and trees of the countries he passed through (as Charlemagne did too), carrying them back to plant in his gardens. Of the ten gardens he laid out in Kabul, the Garden of Fidelity is the one he most loved. Its enclosed formal style was new to India, where the earlier Buddhist gardens were landscapes or groves of trees sacred to the temples they surrounded.

THE MOGUL EMPEROR BABUR SUPERVISING WORKMEN IN THE GARDEN OF FIDELITY (150

England: *"All Nature is a Garden"*

WILLIAM KENT

"CAPABILITY" BROWN

PLAN FOR A "NATURALISTIC" FLOWER GARDEN

VIEW OF SYON HOUSE FROM KEW GARDENS

England's original contribution to garden art is the landscape park. William Kent was among the first to see that "all nature is a garden" and his famous dictum was "Nature abhors a straight line," a pronouncement which dismissed in five words all the magnificent acres of Renaissance gardens. "Unnatural bad taste" the landscape gardeners considered them, and did not hesitate to sweep them away.

"An open country is but a canvas on which a landscape might be designed." So said Horace Walpole. And if Renaissance gardens are most helpfully considered as music, the landscape style should certainly be looked at as painting.

Of these "Improvers of Nature" Capability Brown was the most admired, and his gardens now, two centuries later, are still superb, the trees grown to their full majestic height and the carefully modulated sweeps of grass needing no more maintenance than the grazing of cattle. It was Brown who laid out the part of Kew Gardens known as Syon Vista, scooping out the flat banks of the River Thames to form an artificial lake, piling the earth in little natural-looking hills which he heightened with trees, as we can see in the engraving opposite.

Other designers were less restrained in their tastes. There was Sir William Chambers, for instance, who came back from China to fill his gardens with all kinds of charming Oriental follies like the ones shown here. They were much admired, and the gardens of England came to be studded with Gothick dovecotes, Turkish mosques, temples of Venus, and pedimented gates (to one of these Pope addressed an epigram beginning "Oh gate, how cam'st thou here?"). Fake Gothick ruins were particularly fashionable and a "layout" was not considered complete without a moldering arch.

But these fashionable fancies were not to everyone's taste. In 1778 Lord Lyttleton was moved to protest the "little white edifices" in the famous garden of his cousin, Lord Temple, at Stowe. "Our climate," he wrote, "is not fitted to the deities of Italy and Greece, and in a hard winter, I feel for the shuddering divinities."

ARTIFICIAL RUIN IN THE GARDENS AT KEW

A "GOTHICK GROTTO"

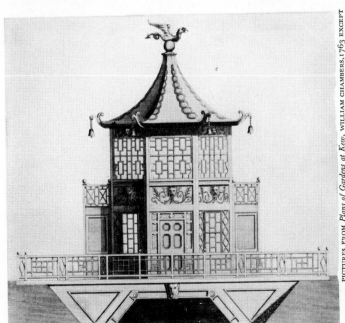

"THE HOUSE OF CONFUCIUS" AT KEW

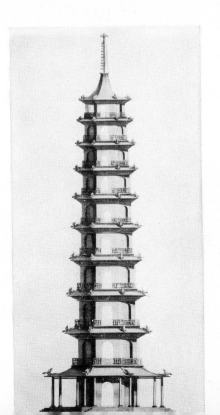

THE "GREAT PAGODA" IN KEW GARDENS

PICTURES FROM Plans of Gardens at Kew, WILLIAM CHAMBERS, 1763 EXCEPT CENTER, The English Garden, RALPH DUTTON, B. T. BATSFORD LTD. 1950

47

Spain and

Portugal:

The Moorish

Influence

THE PLAZA DE LAS FLORES,
CORDOVA, SPAIN. CARNATIONS
AND GERANIUMS BLOOM IN
POTS HUNG ON THE WALLS.

GARDEN OF THE PALACE OF FRONTEIRA, NEAR LISBON, PORTUGAL. POTS OF GERANIUMS ARE PLACED ALONG THE BALCONIES.

The Moors who conquered Spain brought with them the Eastern style of small garden enclosures, and produced in this new environment the most perfect courtyards and gardens, such as the famous ones which still survive at the Alhambra and Generalife. In the kindlier gardening climate of Portugal, Renaissance style from Italy created magnificent gardens like the one above at the Palace of Fronteira. It is much like the Italian creations, though the use of colored faïence on the terrace is Moorish.

These are magnificent showpieces, but the particular and individual charms of Spain and Portugal are the little courtyard gardens, the patios which are more truly rooms for outdoor living than any other gardens had ever been. They have water in wells and pools and fountains. The ground is often paved, with spaces in the paving for growing trees and shrubs, and flowers are set about in pots. Sometimes, as in the little public Plaza de las Flores at Cordova, the surrounding walls, inset with plants, become part of the garden.

This is a form within the range of ordinary people as distinct from Renaissance princes, and it is also well-suited to modern urban living, since the little space the garden covers becomes an outdoor extension of the house. These no doubt are the reasons why it has continued as an unbroken tradition right up to the present day.

JEAN-PHILIPPE CHARBONNIER, COURTESY *Réalités*

THE SAND GARDEN OF THE ZEN BUDDHIST TEMPLE OF RYOAN-JI, KYOTO

WERNER BISCHOF-MAGNUM

STEPSTONES IN KYOTO'S IRIS POND

Japan: Water, Sand, and Stones

Japanese gardening begins in the Chinese fashion which reached Japan with Buddhism in the fifteenth century A.D. The Japanese developed this style in their own way, with a new feeling for restraint and suggestiveness. They evolved elaborate rules for constructing their gardens, and were very skilled at creating landscapes in little. Trees were trained and pruned by gardeners on ladders; paths turned unexpectedly to emphasize vistas; and at the end of a view trees were clipped to give the effect of distance, while nearby shrubs were chosen for their rough texture to make them seem very close. Rocks were given symbolic meanings and greatly prized, and were often brought from long distances, sometimes wrapped in brocade for the journey.

The pond garden was part of the original Chinese style, and from this the Japanese developed the small enclosed level garden, where great care was given to the texture and modeling of the ground. Steppingstones were artfully placed to carry the eye onward; sometimes, when the arrangement of moss and pebbles and water and sand at the walker's feet was considered most important, the stones were set slightly too far apart, to keep attention on the ground.

In this final refinement the level garden became a Zen Buddhist exercise in meditation and self-effacement. It was small and austere and of a deceptive simplicity. It was still in essence a landscape garden, though nature was no longer represented but suggested by symbols. The most famous of these gardens is Ryoan-ji at Kyoto, a temple garden built in 1499. It is composed of fifteen stones, a little moss around the stones, and finely raked sand. Nothing else. The stones are set in groups, and for the Japanese are symbols with many meanings, representing the Buddha and his consorts, the world and its sorrows of war and poverty, the insignificance of man, and the Buddhist ideal of Nothingness. The meaning and beauty depend upon our own perceptions.

50

MOSS TEMPLE GARDEN, SAIHO-JI

EZRA STOLLER—CREATIVE GARDENS, ©1958 REINHOLD

A GARDEN IN BALTIMORE, MARYLAND, SHOWING STRONG JAPANESE INFLUENCE

GOTTSCHO-SCHLEISNER

AN INFORMAL AZALEA GARDEN IN WOODSIDE ACRES, SYOSSET, NEW YORK

America: Gardens to Live In

In garden design the United States has borrowed from many peoples: from the Japanese (in contemporary settings), from the Spanish (in southwestern dwellings), from the English (in formal and estate gardens—now on the wane). Some of the most striking effects have been achieved in great public "wild gardens" like that on the facing page.

In our time a new and original style is being developed in the American private garden. As the pressures of modern life increase and throughways eat into the tulip beds, people look to their gardens for privacy and quiet. Renaissance, Japanese, and English landscape gardens were designed to be seen; contemporary American gardens are for living. A garden today is a place to eat, to recline, to entertain, but not a rolling greensward to stroll upon and admire. As late as the last century, the American garden was laid out comfortably with a front yard and a back yard and was generously exposed to the public view with no enclosing walls. The need for "psychic relief from the machine age" has brought us back to the enclosed garden.

The garden shown at left above is an admirable example of this new trend. While it clearly owes much to the Japanese, it is in no sense a landscape or "natural" garden, an imitation of nature. It is frankly man-made, contrived, strictly controlled to meet specific needs by mechanical devices, not by gardeners. (The pool can be drained to make a patio for entertaining; the pool itself, with lights at night, is an architectural feature of the house which surrounds it.) Such a garden is, really, formal: a little private paradise for the enjoyment of the proprietors. Here we are back where we started more than three thousand years ago, with a garden that is primarily a dwelling place for green things and people, in quiet harmony. The Garden of Eden no longer seems so remote in time; here we have, in essence, a *giardino secreto*, a pleasure garden.

CYPRESS GARDENS WITH AZALEAS
CHARLESTON, SOUTH CAROLINA

A MEMORANDUM

From: Lucius Annaeus Seneca

To: Tennessee Williams

Subject: Horror

This is a fan message. You may never have heard of me: after all, I have been dead a long time. Still, I was, like you, a playwright. Like you, I loved to dominate and to horrify my audiences, and I had considerable success. My dramas have been read, off and on, for nineteen centuries. I saw them all performed during my lifetime, with an emperor as the male lead. Some of my best effects were borrowed by later dramatists, quite shamelessly. Will Shakespeare tells me he thought it was not plagiarism when he did so, but a genuine tribute to an Old Master.

You will meet us in due course, at the Dramatists' Club. We always discuss the new plays and watch the development of promising talents like yours. There are several points I want to argue with you; but meanwhile I must express my admiration for your work. Strikingly original— that is its first and perhaps its greatest merit. Even your titles: *The Glass Menagerie, A Streetcar Named Desire, The Rose Tattoo, Twenty-seven Wagons Full of Cotton, Sweet Bird of Youth.* Superb!

Equally original are your plots. Of course it is difficult to do as I did, to take a story so old that it has been used three hundred times and still to make it into an arresting piece of drama. But I think it must be even harder to invent stories which are apparently brand-new and which (although they sometimes seem crazy) still hold together and leave an indelible impression on the audience. Will used to lift all his plots straight out of history books and anthologies of short stories. He defends this by saying that no dramatist can out-invent life, which is always creating staggeringly new plot-lines. Still, I know he envies you your gift of drawing brilliant ideas out of your own strange experience and fertile invention. So do I.

But I have a bit of advice for you about a special dramatic effect in which you have almost rivaled me: horror. Already you have made your men and women say things on the stage that paralyze your audiences with disgust and abhorrence. But why stop with words? Is it because you are still a little afraid of the public? Don't think of them as human beings. A minor member of our Dramatists' Club calls them *les cochons de payants*, which is vulgar Latin for "those swine the customers." Treat them with the contempt you feel for them. Humiliate them, as you humiliate your characters. Degrade them. You have shocked them by your words. Go further, dear boy: shock them by your actions.

Near the end of the third act of *Streetcar*, Stanley Kowalski, furious with lust, grips the perverted flower Blanche in his arms and forces her toward his bed. Then the music swells out and the curtain comes quickly down. In your next play, keep that curtain up. It will add very little to the running time of the show, and a great deal to its effectiveness. As for actors, it should be easy to find sufficiently agile performers, although for matinees you might have to get an understudy. Consult Equity.

At first a few squeamish spectators may expostulate, and there will be protests from occasional groups representing special interests; but such complaints will soon be drowned under a general wave of enthusiasm. In their own homes, your public watches romantic dramas in which, every evening, several men are struck in the face and body, tortured, and shot to death with guns or stabbed with knives; while at least once a week a girl is ravished or brutalized. I need scarcely mention the popular dramas about werewolves and nonhuman monsters. Once upon a time, perhaps, the effects I suggest might have seemed objectionable. Now they belong to the next stage of dramatic exploration. Be courageous. Innovate.

So, in the second act of *Cat on a Hot Tin Roof*, when Big Daddy realizes that he is dying, riddled with cancer, you should use the wonderful invention of light-pictures to cover the backstage wall with gigantic cancer cells, inhabiting the house that Big Daddy built, living and moving and proliferating. At the end of that same play, the curtain comes down some minutes too soon. It is absurd to have such an appetizing creature as Barbara Bel Geddes or Elizabeth Taylor beseeching a young husband to go to bed and make love to her against his will, and I have noticed some male spectators going away from the theater in fits of laughter,

slapping their knees and pinching their wives and declaring, with many a bold phrase, that the climax was meant to be funny. But, my dear colleague, if you kept the curtain up for ten or fifteen minutes more, you would have a truly serious climax, combining two of your favorite themes, profound male humiliation and savage female hysterics.

You have a marvelous dramatic sense, but you are in danger of blunting it and wasting your creative energy. Let me give you an example from my own experience. In one of my own plays I brought off a powerful climax. An old father cursed his son and prayed God for the son's death. The son was thrown from a runaway chariot. His mangled remains were brought back to his home. On the stage, with infinite grief and remorse, the father picked out the fragments of flesh and bone, put the torn limbs together, and reassembled the shattered body for burial. One of my most successful scenes!

My pupil Nero, after starring in some of my plays, went me one better. He was producing a show about the aeronaut Icarus. Nero had him fall screaming out of the sky, to smash upon the stage with such an impact that his blood bespattered the audience. That is the direction in which you ought to work. You threw away a great opportunity in *Suddenly Last Summer*. I suggest that you rewrite it, using the technique of the flashback and introducing a genuine climax. Instead of merely *hearing* a bemused girl talking about the doom of her perverted cousin, let your audience *see* him on the stage being mobbed, and pulled down, and murdered, and his body being cut up and gnawed to pieces by starving, screaming, naked children.

Yet perhaps you will object that this is too difficult for your theater. I doubt it. Still, if you feel that the stage is too cramped, then use the moving illusions of the lighted screen. For instance, put *Orpheus Descending* into three dimensions. As its last act ends, its lonely hero is being burned to death by a mob leader with a blowtorch. Now, it is not enough for the audience to hear a few unconvincing offstage squeals. On the big motion-picture screen, they could and should see this fine effect carried out to the end, enabling them to have the full dramatic experience. There are even finer possibilities in a play of yours that has not yet been produced, called (with exquisite perversity) *Not About Nightingales*. At the end of this drama, a group of convicts are roasted alive in a prison cell. Your vision of life, which can never be realized in a three-act conversation within one of your conventional theater stages, will be fulfilled on the huge screen when these images of disintegrating humanity share their agony with the spectators, screaming in their ears, scorching before their eyes, shriveling in the long agony of a climax that is both crime and punishment: a hell in which actors and audience and playwright suffer together until their mortal nature disappears into melting metal, thin ashes, searing flame, and the relief of annihilation.

Nero would have loved that.

By GILBERT HIGHET

Appartemens des

Calcedop

Fanarikiose

Acropolis ou
Pointe du
Serrail

Serrail de Seutar

ndre

Sinan klop
du G.S

The Grand

Within its walls the Turkish Sultans sought the

ravelers who arrive in Istanbul by sea have a good view of the Grand Seraglio:
a huddle of low, unprepossessing gray buildings built on a bluff at the point
where the Bosporus and the Golden Horn meet the Sea of Marmara. Nearby, and outbidding it for attention, are the six spectacular minarets of the Blue
Mosque and the great dome and minarets of Hagia Sophia—the ornaments of the

56

Against a seventeenth-century view of the Grand Seraglio are posed some of its inhabitants: (from left) the Grand Vizier, or prime minister of the Sultan; under a monstrous plumed crest, the officer who brought round the bowstring for royal executions; the Chief Black Eunuch; the Ladle-Bearer to the Janissaries; and two women of the harem. Between them and the palace lies the Golden Horn, and to the left are the Bosporus, the Sea of Marmara, and the shores of Asia.

In the background labels: nes du Grand Seigneur — Chambre du Divan — Appartements des Officiers — Entrée du Serrail — le de S.te Sophie — Par

Seraglio

answer to an ancient question: Can absolute power bring absolute bliss?

Istanbul sky line and the great attractions for sight-seers. A tourist who asks about the low gray buildings will be told that they are the Topkapı Museum; with luck, he will also learn that until 1851 this was the Sultans' residence, a palace known to Europeans as the Grand Seraglio. But the chances are that a tourist of no more than average inquisitiveness will never learn that this palace was once more splendid

By MARY CABLE

than Versailles, more bloody than the Kremlin, and, though in Europe, as mysterious to Europeans as the Imperial Palace in Peking. Its extraordinary history shaped millions of lives, from the Arabian peninsula halfway across Europe and the Mediterranean, and took place among brainwashed slaves behind an iron curtain that remained drawn from shortly after the conquest of Constantinople, in 1453, to the middle of the nineteenth century.

The Marmara side of Seraglio Point, a steep, 400-foot ascent, was once guarded by a sea wall built of Byzantine rubble, but the wall is tumbled down now to make way for the railway to Bulgaria, and gypsies and beggars live in the ruins. The other side of the point slopes down to the Golden Horn, which is now a raffish dock area, but in the days of the Sultans was beautiful with palaces and gardens. The unadorned stone buildings of the palace, clustered and sprawled together without aesthetic consideration, suggest a military camp; the tented armies of the Seljuk Sultans must have camped like this as they swept across Anatolia from the Asiatic steppes. To modern visitors the whole palace, inside and out, seems drab and rattletrap, and it is hard to understand how the seventeenth-century French traveler Michel Baudier could have reported, "the baths, halls and galleries of this place surpass in their Magnificence the force of the imagination." Few travelers from the West in those days ever got inside the palace, and fewer still got out again—trespassers anywhere on the premises were beheaded, while trespassers in the harem were skinned alive and their skins tacked to the harem gate. But those who saw it agreed with Baudier: the place was dumbfoundingly splendid.

"Now come with me," said a French ambassador to the court of Suleiman, "and cast your eye over the immense crowd of turbaned heads, wrapped in countless folds of the whitest silk, and bright raiment of every kind and hue, and everywhere the brilliance of gold, silver, purple, silk and satin." Lady Mary Wortley Montagu, who passed that way in 1717 when her husband was a British envoy, wrote that the royal gardeners were so gaily dressed that "at a distance they appeared like a parterre of tulips." Entertained at dinner by a wife of the Sultan, Lady Mary observed among the trinkets her hostess was wearing "200 emeralds, every one as large as a halfcrown piece," and four strings of pearls "every one as large as the Duchess of Marlborough's." The knives were of gold set with diamonds and the tablecloth and napkins were embroidered with silk and gold.

The significant point about the Turkish court seems to be that its dazzle was not created by architecture, which had no particular appeal to a race so recently out of tents in Central Asia, but by the portable grandeur inside the buildings. The silks have worn out, the gold and jewels have been nearly all dispersed, and the Grand Seraglio, where three centuries of extraordinary drama were enacted, comes down to us as a bare, dark stage.

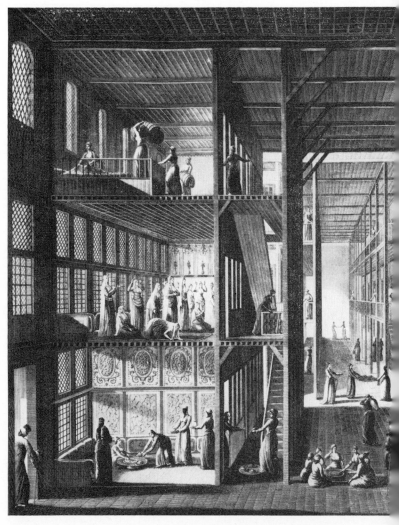

No one now knows exactly what the interior of the harem looked like. The drawing above was made by an architect who, although he could not enter the harem, had many conversations about it with the Sul-

Except for the Sultan and his children, every soul in the Grand Seraglio—even the Grand Vizier, the General of the Armies, and the Queen Mother—was a slave, and not one of them was a Turk by birth. They were brought to the palace as children, between the ages of ten and fourteen. The girls were obtained through slave dealers and the boys, under a law of the land, were kidnapped from subject Christian states in lots of two to three thousand every three or four years. The most intelligent, most prepossessing boys were taken, and their kidnapping was by no means always opposed by their parents, for a place at the Sultan's court was the one available route to wealth and power.

The brightest of these bright children were enrolled in the Palace School inside the Grand Seraglio. Here they underwent a twelve-year brainwashing from which, if they survived, they emerged oblivious of their earlier life, devoted to the sultanate, and fanatical followers of Islam. A seventeenth-century Venetian, Ottaviano Bon, reported of this

tan's sister. In it he tried to introduce all the daily activities of the women, from praying in the mosque (second floor, left) to warming their feet with a rug-covered charcoal brazier (lower right).

school that "There is great severity used in all the orders of discipline, the government of them being in the hands of the masters, who are all white eunuchs for the most part, and very rough and cruel in all their actions; insomuch that when one cometh out of that *Seraglio*, and hath run through all the orders of it, he is, without all question, the most mortified and patient man in the world; for the blows which they suffer, and the fastings which are commanded them for every small fault, are to be admired: nay, some of them are so cruelly handled, that although their time of being in the *Seraglio* be almost expired, and that they should in a few years come forth to be made great men, yet not being able to endure such cruelty any longer, they procure to be turned out, contenting themselves with the title, and small pay of a *Spahee* or a *Mutaferraka* [common soldier] rather than be so often punished and made weary of their lives."

The first thing the new students learned was to keep quiet, for in the inner palace, where the school was, only the Sultan might speak above a whisper. From the Sultan's mutes the boys learned sign languages. "Both the Grand Signor, and divers that are about him," said Bon, "can reason and discourse with the Mutes of any thing as well and as distinctly *alla Mutescha*, by nods and signs, as they can with words; a thing well befitting . . . the gravity of the better sort of Turks, who cannot endure much babbling."

The academic system was excellent, but for the ultimate welfare of the Turkish Empire it had one fatal flaw: it ignored the West. The boys learned Turkish, Arabic, Persian, and Tartar; athletics, riding, and warfare; and a special occupation or skill such as hawk-keeping or turban-folding. According to the Koran, "He who learns is the dearly beloved friend of Allah," and a state law required that every Turk, including the Sultan, should learn how to do something. Mohammed II, the conqueror of Constantinople, was an accredited gardener, and Abdul Hamid II did cabinetwork.

During their training the boys acted as pages. After graduation they became eligible for positions of trust: Private Secretary, Chief Huntsman, Chief Barber, Chief Accountant, Chief Bath Attendant, and so on. If they were gay and amusing fellows, they might become Boon Companions, who hunted with the Grand Seigneur, read to him, and tried to keep him amused. Eventually they might hope to receive the title of pasha and be sent out to govern a province or to spy on some other provincial governor, for the government was a network of spies and counterspies, with the chief officials in a constant welter of plotting against one another and obtaining one another's downfall. "He that is even greatest in office is but a statue of glass," says a Turkish proverb. A popular Turkish curse still is "Mayst thou be vizier to Sultan Selim," for during the eight-year reign of Selim the Grim seven Grand Viziers (prime ministers) lost their heads.

When Sultans decided that this or that vizier must go, their method of dispatching him was often bizarre. Murad IV used to send for the victim, entertain him with a particularly nice feast, and then hand him a black robe and call in the executioner. A number of Sultans gave the condemned man an opportunity to save himself if he could run faster than the executioner from the inner palace to a certain gate on the Marmara shore. If he won the race (he rarely did, most viziers being fat and out of training) he was allowed to keep on going through the gate into exile. Sultan Ahmed I, wishing to dispose of his Grand Vizier, one Nassuf Pasha, sent him two letters by the hand of the Chief Executioner. The first read, "Fail not presently upon the receipt hereof, to send me the Seals of my Empire," the seals being the symbol of his office. Nassuf having handed over the seals, the Chief Executioner gave him the second letter which said, "After that thou hast sent me my Seals, send me thy head by him that shall give thee this note." Michel Baudier, who reported this story in the West, observes, "This command was rough and the style of his letter troublesome, yet he must obey. Nassuf suffered himself to be strangled and the *Bostangibassi* [Head Executioner] carried away his head in the view of all his great family, whereof the least scullions might have broacht him with their spits. Yet no man moved, seeing the people of the Serrail, and knowing that it was the Prince's pleasure."

Heads, whether of viziers or of other slaves, were the usual adornment of the Seraglio's second gate, which was called the Gate of the Executioner. Anyone on legitimate business might enter the first gate, but beyond the Gate of the Executioner no one went except by invitation or duress. At this gate, which leads through a wall some twenty feet thick, modern tourists buy their museum tickets and check their umbrellas. There are a few axes on display, but the fountain where the headsman washed up after work is overgrown with weeds, and there is no sign of the "seventy-seven instruments of torture—nails, gimlets, razors, matches for scorching . . . different powders for blinding, clubs for breaking the hands and feet," which a court historian ascribed to Black Ali, Chief Executioner to Murad IV. Of Black Ali's assistants, the record says, "No light shines from their faces, for they are a dark set of people." Foreign ambassadors arriving to present their credentials were customarily kept waiting at this gate for hours and sometimes days in the society of this agreeable crew.

The Chief Executioner, for a reason whose significance seems to have been forgotten, was also the Chief Gardener and Chief Helmsman of the Royal Caïque, thus combining in his duties the two most striking characteristics of the Ottoman Turk: extreme ferocity and a touching pleasure in the out-of-doors. The Grand Seraglio was surrounded by gardens—not formal ones like those at Versailles and Schönbrunn, but rambling woods and orchards, like English parks, kept in good order by four thousand gardeners. "Nor indeed doth a *Turke* at any time shew himself to be so truly pleased, and satisfied in his senses, as he doth . . . in a pleasant garden," reports Ottaviano Bon. "For, he is no sooner come into it but he puts off his uppermost Coat and lays it aside, and upon that his *Turbant*, then turns up his sleeves and unbuttoneth himself, turning his breast to the wind. . . . Again, sometimes standing upon a high bank to take the fresh air, holding his arms abroad, courting the weather, and sweet air, calling it his soul, his life, and his delight; with whole flowers he stuffes his bosom and decketh his *Turbant*, shaking his head at their sweet favors; and sometimes singing a song to some pretty flower, by whose name peradventure his mistress is called."

The favorite flower of the Turk was the tulip, once a wild flower of the Asiatic steppes. Holland never heard of tulips until 1562, when a shipment of bulbs arrived from Constantinople; the word "tulip" comes from *tulbend*, meaning "turban," a Turkish nickname for the flower. It was said of Ahmed III, a Sultan of the early eighteenth century, that he valued human life less than a good tulip bulb. He devoted himself to importing new varieties from Europe and the Orient and, from Venice, glass vases to put them in. At tulip time every spring official business came to a standstill, while Sultan Ahmed put on all-night tulip fetes in the Seraglio gardens. Guests dressed up in tulip colors, caged birds sang in the tree branches, and here and there among the tulip beds tortoises with candles strapped to their backs provided ambulatory illumination. One particular night of the fete was reserved for the ladies of the harem, who organized a bazaar at which the Sultan was the only customer. They all looked for candy, hidden Easter-egg style among the flowers, and received prizes handed out by the Chief White Eunuch.

White eunuchs came from among the kidnapped slave children and, it appears, chose of their own free will to be castrated in order to obtain certain powerful positions in the palace. Eunuchs were believed to be less corruptible than other people (says Ottaviano Bon: "though not of great courage, yet of the greatest judgment, and fidelity; their minds being set on business, rather than on pleasure") and were thus entrusted with the treasure, the mail, and the secret documents. The governing of the harem was carried on by black eunuchs, most of whom came from the Sudan where they had been captured and castrated as small boys of six or seven. The uglier their faces and persons the more highly they were valued.

Those kidnapped children who showed an aptitude for ferocity were not sent to the Palace School but put into the Janissary Corps. The janissaries were a sort of private army of the Sultan who took the field only when he did and acted as his personal bodyguard. They were first organized in 1330, when the Turks were still living on the plains of Anatolia, and were called *yeni chéri*, meaning "new soldiers." A legend says that a holy man passed his wide sleeve over their heads, blessing them, and for this reason they wore a cap that hung down behind like a sleeve. They were Spartan in their habits, celibate, and forbidden to quarrel with one another. Native Turks and children of former janissaries were not allowed to join the Corps. They were a brave and valuable lot until the great period of Turkish conquests was over and the Sultans became more interested in dallying at home in the Seraglio than in leading troops. Their number swelled from twelve thousand under Suleiman the Magnificent to forty-nine thousand a hundred years later, as more and more captured children entered their ranks and no great wars killed them off. From admirably disciplined assault troops they turned into a rowdy and dangerous mob of hoodlums, always discontented, looting, starting fires, and prone to start revolutions. By 1826, when Mahmud II succeeded in abolishing them, there were 135,000 of them, including many native Turks and sons of janissaries. Six Sultans in two and a half centuries had been

Despite its Italianate style, this is a portrait from life of Mohammed II, the conqueror of
Constantinople and builder of the Seraglio. It was painted by the Venetian Gentile Bellini, 61
who was sent to Constantinople in 1479 at the Sultan's request and spent over a year there.

dethroned or murdered, or both, by the Corps that was supposed to guard them. Lady Mary Wortley Montagu, on her visit to Constantinople in 1717, observed that the Grand Seigneur "trembles at a janissary's frown. [The Turks have] none of our harmless calling names! But when a minister here displeases . . . in three hours' time he is dragged even from his master's arms. They cut off his hands, head, and feet, and throw them before the palace gate, with all the respect in the world; while that Sultan (to whome they all profess an unlimited adoration) sits trembling in his apartment, and dare neither defend nor revenge his favourite. This is the blessed condition of the most absolute monarch upon earth, who owns no *law* but his *will*." Mahmud II plotted for sixteen years to undermine the power of the janissaries, then provoked them into rebellion and used the regular army to destroy them. Twenty-five thousand janissaries died in three days in Constantinople, and that was the end of the Corps.

Janissaries wore long mustachios but no beards. Their rank was shown by the color of their boots— red, yellow, or black. A high-ranking janissary wore a bird-of-paradise plume curving down his back as far as his knees. The Corps emblem was a kettle, and the Chief of Janissaries was titled Head Soup-Distributor. Each man wore in his cap a spoon in a brass socket. Every Friday a large delegation of janissaries came to the second court of the Seraglio, just inside the Executioner's Gate, to get their weekly rice allowance, and if they were disgruntled about anything they would turn their kettles upside down and beat on them with their spoons, a warning to those in the inner palace that somebody's head was wanted.

Janissaries were uneducated except in violence and were fanatically conservative. In 1763, when Lord Baltimore passed through Constantinople, he observed that the Corps was still carrying bows and arrows, sabers and lances, having never got used to firearms. Sultan Selim III, in 1807, was dethroned and murdered during a janissary revolt because he had attempted some reforms, among them the introduction of a printing press into Turkey. Turks had been resisting the printing press ever since it had been invented on the grounds that if the scriptures were printed they wouldn't be scriptures any more.

It is hardly surprising that the Sultan, the Sublime Turk, at the top of this peculiar political structure, was always eccentric, frequently bloodthirsty, and sometimes totally out of his mind. From his solid-gold cradle on, he was the center of lethal intrigue. While he was heir apparent he was in continual danger of being murdered by his younger brothers,

This steamily sensuous view of a Turkish bath by the otherwise cool French classicist J. A. D. Ingres is, needless to say, a work of the imagination. But he based it on the vivid descriptions of that indefatigable traveler Lady Mary Wortley Montagu, who visited several harems in 1717.

who had everything to gain by his death, since the law of the land, the Law of Fratricide, required that when an heir apparent succeeded to the throne he must destroy all his brothers so that there could be no excuse for civil war. Another curious law, the Law of Succession, was borrowed by medieval Turks from the House of Genghis Khan in the warlike days when a Sultan was apt to be killed in battle while still young, leaving only a child heir. This law provided that the inheritance must go first to the eldest member of the royal family and then, on his death, back again to the direct heir. Thus a living brother of the Sultan took precedence over the Sultan's son.

When Mohammed III came to the throne in 1595 he ordered the immediate destruction of his nineteen brothers. As these were all under the age of eleven and had not yet been circumcised, the executioners first circumcised and then strangled them. One child was eating chestnuts when his murderers found him and begged to be allowed to finish them, but his request was not granted. It was unlawful to spill royal blood, so the business was done by strangulation, usually by mutes, with a silken bowstring.

Ahmed I, the son of Mohammed III, was the first Sultan to break the Law of Fratricide. He refused to eliminate his brother Mustafa because Mustafa was half-witted, and all half-wits are, according to the Koran, especially beloved of Allah. Instead of killing him, Ahmed had him shut up in a small, two-story building in the inner regions of the harem, which came to be known as the Cage. When Ahmed died in 1617, Mustafa, under the Law of Succession, inherited the throne. But when it became clear that he was not up to functioning as Sultan, he was put back in the Cage and Ahmed's fourteen-year-old son Osman was enthroned in his place. At once all the civil disorder broke out that the Law of Fratricide had been designed to prevent. The janissaries overturned their kettles, and for six years there was a terrible struggle between factions for Mustafa and factions for Osman. Before order was restored both of them had been murdered.

The next Sultan, Murad IV, who came to the throne at twelve, put things to rights by liquidating four thousand fractious janissaries and closing the coffeehouses, which had become nests of spies and plotters. Prohibition, already a church and state law, he emphasized by pouring boiling lead down the throats of drinkers. He also, for pleasure, used to cut an ass in two with one sword stroke.

This ferocious Sultan was completely under the thumb of his mother, a bloody old lady named

CONTINUED ON PAGE 131

63

The Christian Spaceman—

C. S. LEWIS

An English man of letters,

who made theology entertaining in "The Screwtape Letters,"

now makes it exciting in his novels of planetary adventure

A space ship from Earth has landed on Mars. The hatch opens and three men tumble out. Two of them have been there before, but for Ransom—and for us—it is all new:

The air was cold but not bitterly so, and it seemed a little rough at the back of his throat. He gazed about him, and the very intensity of his desire to take in the new world at a glance defeated itself. He saw nothing but colors—colors that refused to form themselves into things. Moreover, he knew nothing yet well enough to see it: you cannot see things till you know roughly what they are. His first impression was of a bright, pale world—a water-color world out of a child's paint-box; a moment later he recognized the flat belt of light blue as a sheet of water, or of something like water, which came nearly to his feet. They were on the shore of a lake or river.

Ransom is a most unlikely space traveler: a round-shouldered, unathletic philologist from Cambridge. And indeed he is on Mars only because he has been kidnapped by the other two men. Not long afterward he escapes from them and in his flight encounters a being of an unknown kind, rather like a seven-foot otter. Ransom's dread is to some extent conquered by the philologist's curiosity when he hears it making sounds that are unmistakably language, but it is a terrifying moment. Nevertheless, it is "the first tingling intercourse of two different, but rational, species," and not until much later does he have a chance to reflect on his misgivings.

It was only many days later that Ransom discovered how to deal with these sudden losses of confidence. They arose when the rationality of the *hross* tempted you to think of it as a man. Then

it became abominable—a man seven feet high, with a snaky body, covered, face and all, with thick black animal hair, and whiskered like a cat. But starting from the other end you had an animal with everything an animal ought to have—glossy coat, liquid eye, sweet breath, and whitest teeth—and added to all these, as though Paradise had never been lost and earliest dreams were true, the charm of speech and reason. Nothing could be more disgusting than the one impression; nothing more delightful than the other. It all depended on the point of view.

What have we here? Space opera à la Buck Rogers or Flash Gordon? No—not with this style and such subtleties of perception as the fact that we cannot really "see" what we do not know and the two ways of looking at another species. High-quality science fiction, then? Not quite that either. This story forms a category of its own, even though it *is* good science fiction.

The best clue is in the phrase "as though Paradise had never been lost." For indeed this Mars ("Malacandra" to its own people) is an unfallen world. It is described in a book called *Out of the Silent Planet*, the first novel of a trilogy that is continued in *Perelandra* and *That Hideous Strength*. All three are adventure stories in the mode of science fiction. But under the trappings lies something else: Christian theology projected beyond Earth and man, a theology of the universe in the dawn of the space age. This is the work of an extraordinary Englishman, jack-of-a-number of intellectual and artistic trades: C. S. Lewis.

Clive Staples Lewis, to spell him out fully, holds a chair in Medieval and Renaissance English Literature at Cambridge University. The two most specialized of his books are

By EDMUND FULLER

*Narnia, which Lewis created for his children's books,
is a world of unicorns, centaurs, and Talking Beasts.*

the fruits of his scholarly labors: the volume on the sixteenth century in the *Oxford History of English Literature* and *The Allegory of Love*, a medieval study. His other books range from a partial autobiography through a variety of fiction and non-fiction, including a wonderful series for children.

The mainspring of all these writings is the fact that Lewis is a believing Christian (Anglican in affiliation), and his primary fame is as the most imaginative and versatile of Christian apologists.

A few of his books are traditional apologetics, straightforwardly didactic. *Mere Christianity* (developed from a notable series of BBC talks), *Miracles*, and *The Problem of Pain* are good examples and are enough to distinguish him in this field. But for all their merit such books of argumentation would not have built his following and his reputation. His finest apologetics are in the series of fantastic novels which disclose as rich a gift for sheer imaginative writing as our all-too-literal age can boast. Once again the artist and the spinner of tales proves the best persuader.

Lewis was converted to Christianity from atheism. In the nature of such matters, the preparatory processes were prolonged, the moment of actual crossover from no-God to God was abrupt, and the subsequent progression from general theism to specific theology was again a more gradual evolution. He has given us his own account of this history in *Surprised by Joy*. But a sensitive reader will perceive that in the popular *Screwtape Letters* he has also objectively and obliquely described many separate stages of the conversion experience.

He was born in 1898 in Ireland, some touch of which land may have contributed to his gifts as a fantasist. From a home that was nominally religious (Protestant), he went through the mills of education (graphically reported) and emerged an "enlightened" atheist. At nineteen he stumbled upon the book *Phantastes* by the early Victorian mystic George Macdonald. Of that experience he testifies:

My imagination was, in a certain sense, baptized; the rest of me, not unnaturally, took longer. I had not the faintest notion what I had let myself in for by buying *Phantastes*. I met there all that had already charmed me in Malory, Spenser, Morris, and Yeats. But in another sense all was changed. I did not yet know (and I was long in learning) the name of the new quality, the bright shadow, that rested on the travels of Anodos. I do now. It was Holiness.

The conversion seeded by Macdonald, and watered later by G. K. Chesterton and a variety of personal relationships, flowered at Oxford when Lewis was thirty-one: "That which I greatly feared had at last come upon me. In the Trinity Term of 1929 I gave in, and admitted that God was God, and knelt and prayed; perhaps, that night, the most dejected and reluctant convert in all England."

Except for service in World War I in which he was wounded (he first read Chesterton in an army hospital), Lewis has led a wholly academic life, sharing his home with his older brother. Among his friendships, two undoubtedly combine both religious and literary influences. These have been with the late Charles Williams and with J. R. R. Tolkien, both of whom are masters of the fantastic and have used it as a vehicle for religious concepts. A few years ago he married an American, Joy Davidman, herself a talented poet and novelist, and also a convert (in part through the influence of Lewis's writings, long before meeting him).

C. S. Lewis shows us reality through fantasy and symbol which, as the mythmakers and poets always have known, are the closest approaches to elusive reality that we can make. The reality structure he offers us is that proclaimed by Christianity. To the Christian it is truth, to the non-Christian a tale.

Modern fiction is dominated by what is called "realism" or, in its most literal form, "naturalism." It glories in its imitation of the technique of reporting. The claim to "realness" lies in the fact that many things (including an unstinting catalogue of revolting things) which people in fiction are portrayed as doing are indeed done by people in life. In itself, this coincidence does not in any way assure the over-all "reality."

Attempts to portray the reality of life (which can only be approximate at best) succeed to the degree to which they manage to capture and reflect glimpses of the total reality of who we are, what we are, and where we are. The error of confining literature to what is mistakenly called "realism" is to suppose that what we see, hear, feel, taste, smell, or think can be dignified by so presumptuous a word as "real." At the most it is a fragment of reality, as the mystic and the physicist alike can testify.

In one of Lewis's books for children there is a conversation about a star. "In our world," a boy says, "a star is a huge ball of flaming gas." He is answered: "Even in your world, my son, that is not what a star is but only what it is made of." The attempt to equate a human being with the wretched few pennies' worth of chemical elements of which our substance is composed is likewise an answer to the pseudo realists.

Possibly the most famous of Lewis's single works is the little volume called *The Screwtape Letters*. With wit and grace it ranges over a wide swath of Christian thought by the device of seeing it from the enemy camp. It is a series of letters from a minor administrative devil, Screwtape, to his nephew, a junior tempter named Wormwood, advising him on the campaign for the soul of the human being to whom Wormwood has been assigned. The inexperienced tempter is counseled not to let his subject acquire

the fatal habit of attending to universal issues and withdrawing his attention from the stream of immediate sense experiences. Your business is to fix his attention on the stream. Teach him to call it "real life" and don't let him ask what he means by "real". . . . Keep pressing home on him the *ordinariness* of things.

Man urgently needs for his intellectual and spiritual health the recovery and preservation of wonder, awe, radical amazement, the sense of the Holy. We require the breaking down of what Lewis calls "our nature's incurable incredulity," for it is the vulgar error of our day to believe too little rather than too much. The real fool is he who is so afraid of being gulled that he will permit himself no belief. Accordingly, many of us have

eased the burden of intolerable strangeness which this universe imposes on us by dividing it into two halves (natural and supernatural) and encouraging the mind never to think of both in the same context.

The "realist" invokes the "laws of Nature" against the "miraculous." But

the Laws of the universe are never broken. Your mistake is to think that the little regularities we have observed on one planet for a few hundred years are the real unbreakable laws.

Chad Walsh, in the only book-length study of Lewis and his work to date, called him "Apostle to the Skeptics." With equal aptness, he is Apostle to the Space Age. He uses the resources of contemporary imagination, blended freely with motifs from classical mythology, as vehicles for eternal inquiries. Lewis sees in mythology "the childhood of religion . . . a prophetic dream"; Christianity fulfills "the hints of all Paganism. . . ." Thus his wonderful perception of why, inevitably, in a fallen world, "mythology was what it was—gleams of celestial strength and beauty falling on a jungle of filth and imbecility."

To see his methods in operation, we should examine the trilogy that begins with *Out of the Silent Planet*. Taken at no other level than pure, enthralling adventure these are first-class stories, exuberantly inventive and especially notable for the descriptive evocation of strange worlds.

The universe of Lewis is not the chilling wilderness of "space." To his hero, Ransom, bathed in the fearful glory between the worlds,

the very name "Space" seemed a blasphemous libel. . . . He could not call it "dead". . . . Since out of this ocean the worlds and all

In The Silver Chair, *one of the Chronicles of Narnia, Prince Rilian overcomes the evil Witch of Underland.*

their life had come. He had thought it barren: he saw now that it was the womb of worlds. . . . No: Space was the wrong name. Older thinkers had been wiser when they named it simply the heavens.

The overwhelming distances of astronomy, which leave the human helpless in the presence of immensity, Lewis wraps in the term "deep heaven." His universe is not lifeless, hostile, empty, or impersonal. It is the whole created realm of God, harmonious in the Great Dance, which is the motion of galaxies and stars and of all things, great and small, atom and organism. Some places in this universe are inhabited by beings analagous to man (as astronomy also believes), but elsewhere and everywhere by beings of other and higher orders—that complex hierarchy known alike to Christian, Jew, and Moslem as angels. Not to believe in this hierarchy is to presume a one-jump gap in powers and natures between man and God. Earth is one of the "low worlds." The great planets, Jupiter and Saturn, are the province of mighty, intelligent beings who are not organisms.

But at the opening of the trilogy Ransom does not know all this. On a hiking tour he blunders into the hands of a sinister pair named Weston and Devine, and the great adventure begins. Professor Weston is a physicist of genius who has built a space ship. He represents the man-centered materialist to whom religion is superstition; his goal is no less than the colonization of the universe by man and the perpetuation of genus Homo. Devine, his financial backer and partner, is interested only in a cash return and embodies ruthless greed. Together they have already made one successful trip to Malacandra (Mars) and are about to embark on another. But they need a specimen of man to give to the ruler of that planet, they think for human sacrifice, and Ransom fortuitously becomes their intended victim.

The title *Out of the Silent Planet* is a clue to the meaning. Ransom, to whom the strange planet is at first a scene of terror, eventually realizes that the true place of horror is the world from which he has come, which is known on

TEXT CONTINUED ON PAGE 125

On following page: a scene from Perelandra

ON ANOTHER PLANET, ANOTHER EVE

A passage from the novel PERELANDRA

The water gleamed, the sky burned with gold, but all was rich and dim, and his eyes fed upon it undazzled and unaching....One of the great patches of floating stuff was sidling down a wave. . . . From its tawny surface a whole series of feathery and billowy shapes arose, very unequal in height . . . an island if you like, with hills and valleys, but hills and valleys which changed places every minute so that only a cinematograph could make a contour map of it. And that is the nature of the floating islands of Perelandra . . . for they are dry and fruitful like land but their only shape is the inconstant shape of the water beneath them. . . .

Over his head there hung from a hairy tube-like branch a great spherical object, almost transparent, and shining. . . . And looking round he perceived innumerable shimmering globes of the same kind in every direction. . . . Each of the bright spheres was very gradually increasing in size, and each, on reaching a certain dimension, vanished with a faint noise, and in its place there was a momentary dampness on the soil and a soon-fading, delicious fragrance and coldness in the air. In fact, the things were not fruit at all but bubbles.

As his country climbed the smooth mountains of dimly lustrous water he had frequent opportunity to see that many other islands were close at hand. . . . It was a wonder to see these big mats or carpets of land tossing all around him like yachts in harbor on a rough day—their trees each moment at a different angle just as the masts of the yachts would be.

He was tortured with the fear that the distance between the islands might be increasing. Thank God: here came the orange land over the crest following him down into the pit. And there was the stranger, now on the very shore, face to face with him. . . . Was *this* what he had been sent to meet? He had been expecting wonders, had been prepared for wonders, but not prepared for a goddess carved apparently out of green stone, yet alive. And then it flashed across his mind—he had not noticed it while the scene was before him—that she had been strangely accompanied. She had stood up amidst a throng of beasts and birds as a tall sapling stands among bushes—big pigeon-colored birds and flame-colored birds, and dragons, and beaver-like creatures about the size of rats, and heraldic-looking fish in the sea at her feet. . . . From a wood of bubble-trees behind her half a dozen creatures like very short-legged and elongated pigs—the dachshunds of the pig world—were waddling up to join the assembly. Tiny frog-like beasts, like those he had seen falling in the rain, kept leaping about her. . . . Amidst all this she stood looking at him . . . her stare level and unafraid, communicating nothing.

Venus is called "Perelandra" in the novels of C. S. Lewis. Under its eternal mantle of clouds he imagines it as a place of endless oceans, floating islands, and diffused golden light. And the green woman his hero encounters there is not the Aphrodite of this watery world, but its Eve.

PAINTING BY JAMES LEWICKI

SURPRISE
IN THE
SAHARA

A French expedition discovers astonishing murals made by

Stone Age herdsmen in a desolate area that once was green

Early in the 1930's geologists, paleontologists, and archaeologists established that the trackless wastes of the Sahara had once been verdant savannas where men hunted animals in great numbers and tended their herds and crops. The evidence lay in rock strata, fossil remains, and stone artifacts that are plain reading to these experts. But as early as 1909 far clearer evidence, which could be read by anyone with eyes to see, had begun to turn up. In that year a French officer, Captain Cortier, had come out of the Sahara with a report that he had seen a painted bison in a cave high on the great, arid Tassili plateau, 900 miles south of the Mediterranean in Algeria.

From time to time since then marvelous tales have been told by the rare travelers who ventured into this desolate land, one of the least known on earth. They described beautiful paintings on the rock walls of caves and declivities, depicting a profusion of animals that had not inhabited those regions for centuries—the hippopotamus, for instance, whose aquatic habitat testified to the once-lush state of this desert. But the remoteness of the Tassili, its tortuous landscape, and the warlike disposition of the nomadic Tuareg who people it, for many years kept scholars from attempting a systematic study.

Then in 1933 Henri Lhote, a young French scholar-explorer, visited Lieutenant Brenans, an officer of the Camel Corps, who had seen and sketched several of these paintings.

Recognizing their importance, Lhote's imagination was fired and he undertook his first forays into the Tassili plateau. Before he could accomplish much the war intervened. But always he dreamed of the lunar landscape of the high desert and the murals of the Stone Age Africans.

Finally in 1956 Dr. Lhote was able to organize and lead an expedition to the Sahara under the sponsorship of Paris's Musée de l'Homme. For sixteen months he and his team of artists lived on the Tassili plateau, enduring marrow-freezing cold, tearing winds, the incursions of vipers and scorpions, and short rations. There Lhote compiled the first study of the prehistoric paintings, which he believed to have been made between about 8000 and 3000 B.C., while the artists scrupulously copied 400 of the thousands they discovered. Upon their return to Paris the results were exhibited at the Musée des Arts Décoratifs in the Louvre and hailed as one of the major artistic sensations of years, demonstrating the extraordinary quality of this heretofore unknown legacy from our primitive ancestors. On the following pages HORIZON presents an account of the expedition, its trials, and its findings, which were selected from Henri Lhote's book, *A la découverte des fresques du Tassili*, in a translation by Willard Trask. The book itself will be published in the United States this fall by E. P. Dutton & Co. A portfolio of outstanding Saharan rock paintings, in color gravure, begins on page 73.

tents of the Lhote expedition at one of its desert camps are dwarfed
rock formations stretching endlessly across the Tassili plateau.

DISCOVERING A STONE AGE MUSEUM

By HENRI LHOTE

What, after all, is the Tassili? The structure of the massif —500 miles long and from 30 to 35 wide—varies greatly from one section to another. Its southern edge drops abruptly to the Hoggar peneplain from heights of 1,500 to 1,800 feet. The mass of friable sandstone of which it is composed curves in from south to north and gives the same general direction to the valleys. Numerous canyons have been hollowed out by water, growing deeper in proportion to their distance from the ridges. But the work of the water did not end here. It attacked the entire massif, and streaming down, literally sliced into its mass, cut it up in the most fantastic way, eroding, polishing, drilling, in some places changing enormous blocks of stone into lacework. Water? In a country where it almost never rains?

Yes, water. But of course in a very distant past, for these masses of sandstone have been where they are for millions of years, exposed to the elements, and all this spectacular erosion is not the work of yesterday.

It was in this unreal setting that we traveled; the ponderous caravan defiled between tall columns that suggested the ruins of a great medieval city with its crumbling keeps, its church spires, its cathedral porches, its strange signboards representing allegorical animals, its architectural forms each more fantastic than the last. After three days of travel we came to the corrie of Ti-n-Bedjedj.

And what did we see on the walls of the natural shelters that were all about us? Human beings represented in different styles, some with profiles of a European type, others with schematized round heads, yet others with only a little stick for a head. And among the animals that also have a considerable place in this prehistoric museum, we noticed giraffes, cattle, horses drawing war chariots, others ridden

by men armed with javelins, wild sheep being hunted by dogs, and so on. There was no doubt of it: in more favorable times numerous human groups must have frequented the place, and each group had left records of its history after its fashion, in accordance with particular interests—hunting for some, cattle raising for others, war for yet others. What a contrast to the desert setting all around us!

Now for the first time we set up our tents and organized camp for a long stay, for it was here that our work would really begin.

At Tan-Zoumaïtak there was a big shelter with paintings that were already known, but the photographs of them that had been taken previously gave but a poor idea of their artistic quality. When we entered (it is more a cave than a shelter) we were spellbound by what was before us: great human figures painted in yellow ochre, the bodies and hair stippled with white; big wild sheep in white and purplish ochre; white animals outlined with yellow ochre of such curious and imaginative forms that they were almost indeterminable; various other human figures, and a quantity of smaller animals. The whole was in an excellent state of preservation, and we could not stop admiring the unusual forms, the quality of the coloring. Without any doubt it was a miniature Lascaux of the Sahara.

Recording this incomparably fine piece in its entirety demanded the utmost attention to small details and all the skill of our painters. It took almost two weeks and required the efforts of the entire team. As the days passed, our relations with the prehistoric artists of the Tassili became nothing short of a living conference.

At Tamrit, an hour's journey from Tan-Zoumaïtak, the setting was superb, and decidedly different from anything

TEXT CONTINUED ON PAGE 81

On the following eight pages HORIZON presents in gravure a selection of rock paintings discovered on the Tassili plateau of the Sahara, as they were faithfully copied by the Lhote expedition. The awesome figure on the facing page was named "The Great Martian God" because of its resemblance to the characters of outer-space fiction. Found at the Sefar site, it towers eighteen feet high and is the largest prehistoric figure painting known. Something of the difficulty of transposing these astonishing works may be gathered from the photograph at left. One of the artists is wedged into the sort of cramped position they frequently had to endure for hours. First a tracing was made of the outlines of the figures. This was transferred to a background painted to correspond to the rock wall. When distortions had been corrected, the figures were colored after the originals.

The fresco named "The Great Giraffe" (left) was discovered at Adjefou. Six strata of paintings are discernible. The roundheaded figures in red ochre date from the oldest Tassili period. Superimposed are other roundheaded figures in purplish ochre, the string figure, the yellow figure, the giraffe, and finally the antelope of the Bovidian painters, who are thought to have had a median date about 3500 B.C. The stylized masked heads (right) were found at Sefar. Though they resemble Negro African masks, Henri Lhote suggests that they show the Egyptian influence seen in other Tassili paintings. Below, a fresco from Aouanrhet shows what appears to be a village plan. In the region of the Niger such straw huts with an enclosing wall can still be seen. These seem to be joined to the village square by footpaths.

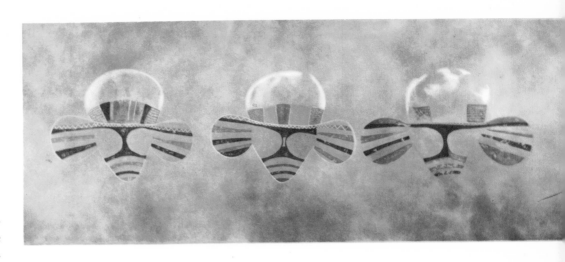

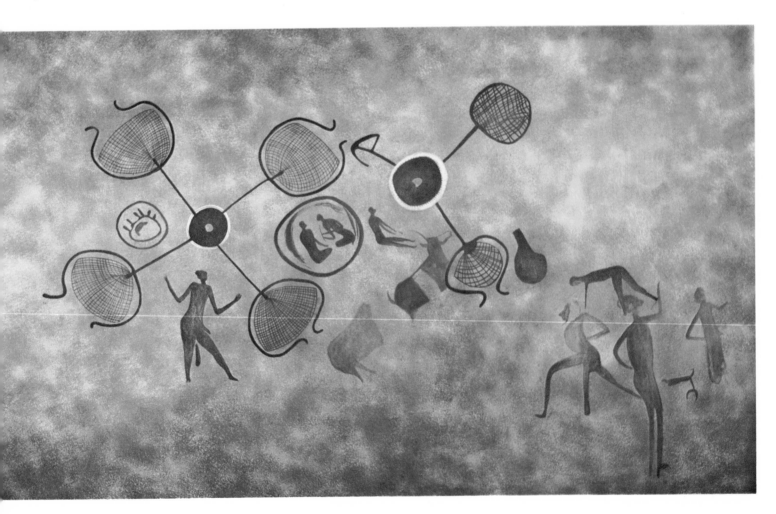

The painting on the next two pages is the most perplexing discovered by the expedition. Named "The Swimming Woman" by the artists, it shows a woman with elongated limbs, and breasts on her back, who appears to be towing a man through a liquid medium. This man, apparently dead, is in a fetal position. Below, another man, with arms thrust forward, emerges from a snail-like object. In the light of certain Egyptian features, Lhote speculates that some ideas of birth and the journey of the dead may be represented here.

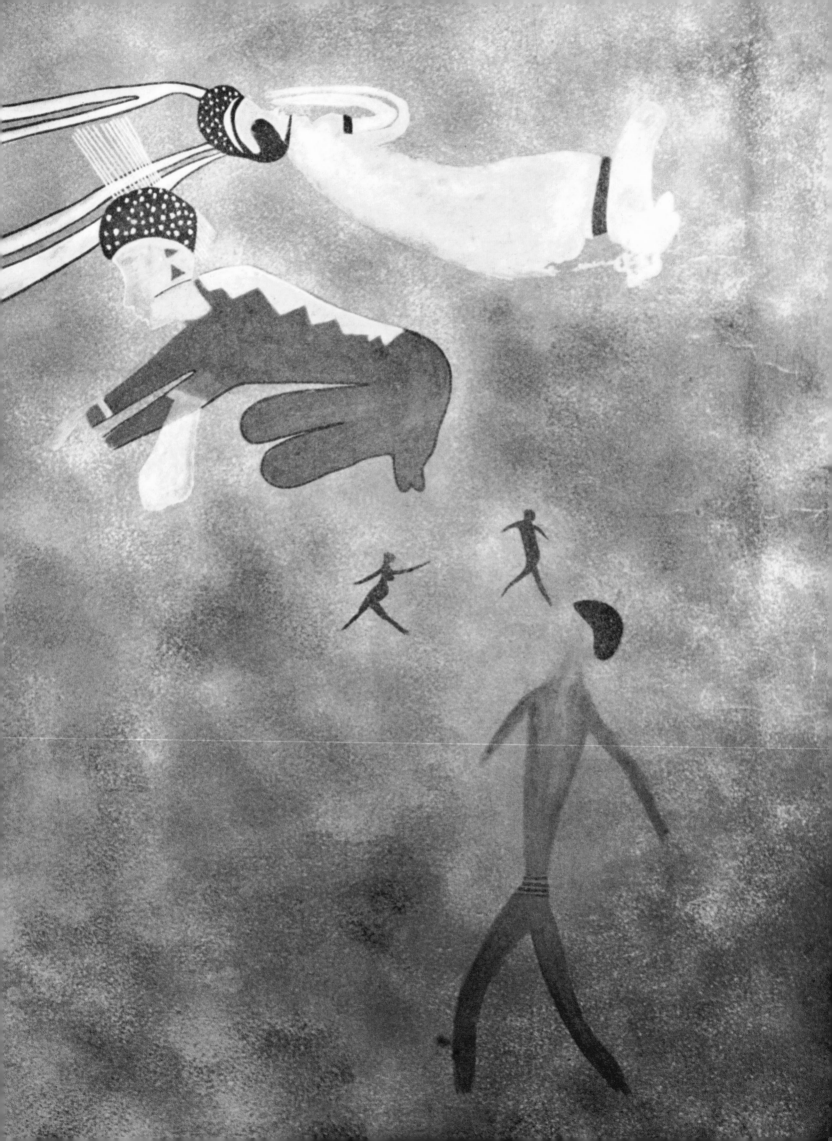

At first the painting at right, copied at Tamrit, seems to represent some monstrous serpent encircling struggling men. But this work closely resembles rock paintings of the predynastic epoch found along the Upper Nile, and the serpent motif seems to be combined with the representation of a Nile River boat. It provides further testimony of Egyptian contacts with the Bovidian artists.

A war chariot is shown in this damaged painting at left from Tin Abou Teka. The six reins indicate that it was drawn by three horses. Although more than 300 chariot paintings have been found in the Sahara, only two others show three horses. These are drawn in the "flying gallop" style characteristic of Cretan paintings of the pre-Roman age. Egyptian chronicles of the Eighteenth Dynasty attest to the use of the chariot by Saharan peoples.

A vast catalogue of Tassili styles and epochs is embodied in the mural above, which measures 27 feet in length and was found at Sefar. Lhote distinguishes twelve successive stages in it. The earliest is represented by the roundheaded, human figures painted in purplish ochre. This type, found widely scattered in the Tassili, belongs to the earliest period of these Saharan paintings which Lhote considers are probably 10,000 years old, or early Neolithic. In later periods there were painted on top of these figures the wild sheep in white with red ochre outlines, elephants, a giraffe, other wild sheep in yellow with red outlines, and the strange white human figures with slender limbs. Finally, a war scene depicting people armed with bows was added by artists of the Bovidian people. The peculiar fact that these last are women who appear to have but one breast has caused Lhote to wonder if they depict female warriors who mutilated themselves in order to draw a bow with ease.

TEXT CONTINUED FROM PAGE 72

we had encountered before. We were settled in shallow caves overlooking the deeply embanked wadi, which was encumbered by enormous slides that made it impossible for camels to pass through. There was still a shallow pool thirty feet from our camp, which gave us an easy supply of the water indispensable for cooking and washing. Most exceptionally, a number of magnificent cypresses whose trunks measured more than eighteen feet in girth rose at intervals from the bed of the wadi, their green foliage making a curious contrast to the brick-red color of the surrounding rocks. Our Tuareg were encamped in a corrie, close to the fires. Five hundred yards away we had the surprise of finding the most striking waterfall in the Tassili, almost 1,800 feet high, with little silvery lakes lying at its foot. This particularly evocative setting allowed us to imagine what life here was like in prehistoric times, when painters beautified these rock walls with hunting scenes or traveling herds of cattle.

And very often in the evening, when our day's work was done and we ourselves had emerged from the shelters that every day yielded us new images, we pictured the grassy valleys, the forest galleries, the pools, and all the animals that had long ago lived in this Eden; into the setting we

The refinement of drawing and anatomical mastery of the Tassili painters are nowhere more splendidly expressed than in the work on the opposite page, found and copied at Jabbaren. The profiles of the two girls are not Negroid, but suggest the women of the Peul tribe. Their arms and hands are treated in a manner resembling that of certain Egyptian paintings of the Eighteenth to Nineteenth Dynasties and the dresses they wear look like those of that period. Below, Henri Lhote is seen in the terrain of the expedition he led.

summoned the placid elephants, gathering at the waterside and waving their great ears, the timid rhinoceroses following the narrow trails that led to their lairs, the giraffes burying their heads in the mimosa, the antelope and gazelles moving in herds from valley to valley pasturing as they went or resting in the shade of the trees. Finally, we imagined the men who lived in the shelters under the rocks, getting their weapons ready for the hunt, making their skin clothing; their women busily cooking, going to wash their pots and to bathe themselves in the nearby watering place. We imagined the herders watching over their cattle in the grasslands, leading their animals to water, driving them back to camp at night and shutting them in behind barricades of branches, safe from beasts of prey.

The paintings were often located on the ceilings of shelters nine feet from the ground, which made it necessary to use ladders; in other cases they were in very low shelters, which meant working on all fours in the most uncomfortable position. The wind tore not only the tracing sheets but also the drawing paper, thus sometimes destroying in a few seconds the result of several days' labor. Nevertheless the most difficult and delicate work was to arrive at the right conception of the images, which were often very much blurred or partly destroyed. There was only one remedy: washing the wall to get rid of the clay dust that had accumulated during the course of millenniums, then freshening the colors by moistening them with vegetable sponges soaked in water. By the naked eye or with the aid of a lens every inch was reconstructed. But at this rate we spent many days over the same painting; the more so as we had to take into account the extreme variations in lighting. It was this repeated washing of walls that was to result in some of our finest discoveries, since some of the paintings were totally invisible to the naked eye under their coating of dust.

The people of the Tassili had the decorative sense and obviously must have known how to paint. But *why* did they paint?

It is generally assumed that prehistoric art was inspired by magical practices; in short that it was born of religion. Its existence in France and Spain, in deep dark caves resembling true sanctuaries, only strengthened the theory, and there is no doubt that the sorcerer in the Trois Frères cave and the decapitated bear in the cave at Montespan can only have had a magical character. Art for art's sake, according to this theory, did not exist and must have been an invention of men who had reached a high stage of evolution. Yet this rule must have been subject to exceptions, for certain painted or engraved subjects apparently have no mystical element and certainly seem to be the product of pure imagination.

I must point out that the variety of our discoveries was very great, and that at least sixteen different strata can be distinguished, corresponding to different styles and periods, each having its particular characteristics. There is no doubt that we found figures that must have represented gods or sorcerers, but there are also groups in which it certainly seems that artists endowed with great imagination must have painted for the sheer pleasure of reproducing what they had before their eyes.

Such is the case, I believe, though certain reservations have to be made with the paintings of the period that we have named "Bovidian,"—that in which domestic cattle appear and which holds a considerable place in the art of the Tassili and first place on the basis of numerical preponderance.

This stratum is the latest of the sixteen to which I referred, for its figures are always superimposed on those of the other strata; on the other hand, it is earlier than the period when the horse is represented, but that is not prehistoric.

In curious and exceptional contrast to other prehistoric artists, the Bovidians always engraved their subjects before painting them. I found a number of sketches that by the multiplicity of their lines would suggest the trial drawings of a modern artist. The lines were extremely fine, as if they had been drawn with a flint. Several such engraved figures had already begun to be filled in with ochre.

The human figures, in the most varied costumes, likewise present fascinating forms full of balance and elegance. Their attitudes reflect motion first and foremost, and we find them in athletic poses: drawing the bow at game, meeting in the battles that were fought for the possession of herds, or gathered together in scenes of dancing.

The representations of domestic occupations are also very numerous and provide a lively picture of their home life. They lived in conical huts; the women crushed grain on grinding stones; and they traveled sitting astride their cattle, the woman riding behind the man.

Were they Negroes or whites? The profiles astonished us by their diversity; some are prognathous, others European-Caucasoid, which suggests that they were not all of one physical type but that several races lived side by side, perhaps as the Tuareg and their Negro slaves do today. The variety of their costumes, which include long tunics, short loincloths, clothing made of fiber, and so on, would corroborate this point of view.

However, the most common type suggests the Ethiopian profile. It was certainly the East that sent out these great waves of pastoral peoples who overran not only the Tassili but the entire Sahara as well. The Bovidian peoples, who appear to have worshiped cattle that sometimes bore an attribute between their horns, were at one time in contact with Egyptian civilization. On five occasions we found among the frescoes reproductions of the Egyptian Nile boat, a decisive element which certainly tends to confirm their Eastern origin.

The expedition moved on to Jabbaren, a day's journey away. In the language of the Tuareg, *Jabbaren* means "the giants," and the name is due simply to the presence there of

prehistoric paintings in which some of the human figures are literally gigantic. In a deep shelter with a curved ceiling one of these figures (*page 73*) measures eighteen feet in height. Without any doubt it is one of the largest prehistoric paintings so far discovered. One has to stand at such a distance to distinguish the forms that it was only after having passed it many times that we realized what we had before us. The outline is simple, without art, and the round head, in which the painter has indicated only one detail—a double oval in the center of the face—suggests our commonly accepted image of the Martians. If the Martians ever set foot in the Sahara, it must have been many centuries ago, since these paintings of roundheaded people in the Tassili are, so far as we know, among the oldest.

Jabbaren was a whole world: more than 5,000 painted subjects in a quadrilateral area measuring scarcely 600 yards on a side! If we consider the different strata of paintings, it follows that more than twelve different civilizations succeeded one another here. It was unparalleled, and considering its area the Tassili can be regarded as the richest prehistoric art center in the world.

The majority of the wall paintings were the work of the Bovidians. There were cattle everywhere—of all styles, in all positions, and the execution was always of remarkable quality. Among many others, Jabbaren held one particularly great surprise in store for us. In the course of washing a rock wall, we noted the presence of four small bird-headed women, absolutely identical with those appearing on certain Egyptian monuments. They were so characteristic that we waited for the usual explanatory hieroglyphics to appear. Despite repeated washings we saw nothing more.

That night in camp the talk was animated and my companions assailed me with questions. Was it possible that the forces of the Pharaohs had pushed on as far as the Tassili? Our little bird-headed goddesses belong to the historical period, perhaps to the Eighteenth or Nineteenth Dynasty, which puts them at about 1200 B.C. Perhaps when the Egyptians conducted a punitive campaign in the Libyan country they pursued some bands as far as their refuges in the Tassili? It is not impossible, though it remains doubtful. In any case, no Egyptian chronicle mentions any such expeditions.

Then how are the paintings to be explained? Two more justifiable hypotheses may be entertained. Either the authors of the paintings were Egyptian prisoners or travelers brought to the Tassili and inspired by the surrounding paintings, or we may be dealing with the work of Libyans who had lived in Egypt of their own free will or as prisoners and had become impregnated with Egyptian culture and, on their return, had brought with them the art of the Nile valley. Then again, centuries of constant fighting between Libyans and Egyptians might suffice to explain the influences. Perhaps our future investigations will contribute more definite data for the Egyptologists who will study the problem.

On the rocks at Adjefou I noticed two quite well-preserved reproductions of chariots. Chariots were nothing new to us. For we had made copies of eight of them during our very first trips into the Tassili.

But the chariots at Adjefou had a particular interest. They were the most oriental of the painted chariots so far discovered, and I emphasize the word "painted," for there are others farther eastward, in Fezzan itself, but they are *engraved* in the rock and were discovered in 1933 by Italian archaeologists.

A little later, in the course of a scouting trip in the Ala-n-Edoument region, I was to find a new chariot painted in red ochre and kaolin, which figured not in a war scene but in a scene of antelope hunting (*page* 79). This whole group of reproductions of war chariots is of the highest interest. It is known that about 1200 B.C. peoples coming from Crete with the intention of attacking Egypt had landed and had mixed with the Libyans. It could be surmised that after the failure of their campaigns against Egypt, these invaders of Cretan origin (actually they seem to have come from much farther away—perhaps from northern Europe, for the Egyptians represented them with the blue eyes characteristic of the Nordic races) had fallen back toward the Sahara, where they must ultimately have mixed with their Libyan allies.

At Sefar we set to work on an astonishing fresco (*pages* 78-79), which proved to be the most complex that we had encountered. Situated in a low-roofed shelter with a sandy floor, it was more than twenty-seven feet in length. Examining it, we discovered that it included twelve strata of paintings corresponding to as many different periods.

We sprinkled the wall with water to bring up the coloring and tried to find the best lighting. For we soon discovered that light entering from the right would bring out a particular red ochre or a particular yellow ochre, while light from the left would bring out the whites or the greenish tones instead, so that we had to return to the same area of the painting ten times at different hours of the day. Finally these repeated checks brought us into agreement.

In our fresco we found more of the little human figures in purplish ochre that seemed to belong to the earliest style. Yet the outstanding representations were the wild sheep, painted in white and outlined in red ochre, which extended in a long line from one end of the fresco to the other. There were also elephants, a giraffe, and more wild sheep belonging to a different period. Painted in yellow ochre and outlined in red, they were distinguished by long tufts of hair at their withers and hoofs. They belonged to the same artistic school as the roundheaded people of Martian type rendered in the same colors, two examples of which occurred in precisely this fresco. Superimposed were human figures painted in white, with long slender limbs. One of them offended Michel, who accused me of making him copy "immoral" scenes! Finally, above, there was a war scene

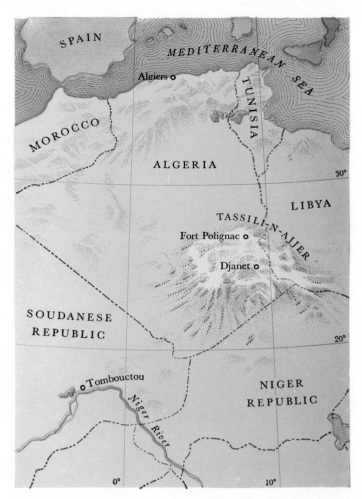

The campsites of the Lhote mission lay high on Tassili-N-Ajjer plateau between Fort Polignac and Djanet, from which they were supplied.

representing people armed with bows, and belonging to the stratum of cattle herders.

To my stupefaction, I observed that these warriors were really women and that each of them had only one breast. We had found no female archers before, so these added to our documentation of the astonishing Bovidians. But the single breast—was it only an appearance suggested by the drawing, or was it the consequence of actual excision. Could the cattle herders have had their Amazons?

The fresco of the "Little Wild Sheep" (for so we named it) was a most valuable lesson for us. Through it we were able to establish a relative chronology, this time applying to twelve strata. This in addition to our earlier observations would enable us to arrive at a more accurate idea of the evolution of prehistoric art in the Tassili. Our joy (and perhaps for me the greatest joy of my life in the Sahara), which is at the same time our reward, is to have entered today in the pages of history a unique document: the thousand-year-old message left by these people and unknown until now, a message of life, a message of art, and a message of the universality of man, which must profoundly move us all.

By WILLIAM HARLAN HALE

Out of the Gargoyles and into the Future

Yale declares an architectural revolution. What will this do to the Ivy League?

We men of Yale, from current students and mentors to oldest living alumni, think of ours as an institution not to be outpaced by any—particularly not by Harvard. Over the generations this Eli drive has embraced campus architecture no less than sports. When Tudor Gothic was the vogue for collegiate building, no university became more moated, turreted, and crenelated than did our own. When academic taste next veered to the neo-Georgian, few establishments of the higher learning remotely approached ours in the speed and cost with which we converted to 1935 model Adam. In my own years at Yale, which saw the transition from one style to the other, we even accomplished that unique creation, Davenport College—a building all Gothic on one side and all red-brick Colonial on the other. Harvard has produced no wonder of the academic world to equal that.

And now that contemporary architecture has achieved its breakthrough on the American campus, Yale has stolen a march on the competition again. In my time I was a brash campus radical who denounced our New Haven "girder Gothic" and cried out (then without success) for buildings in a "living style"; but I never imagined just how lively our style would get, once we broke through. For although Harvard can boast of a stark and somewhat forbidding example of the functional method in the Graduate Center designed by Walter Gropius, we now have something far more avant-garde at Yale in Eero Saarinen's new hockey rink—one of the most exuberant structures put up anywhere in the United States in the name of modernity.

As sage and serious Harvard men have been quick to point out, it would be just like their sister college down along Long Island Sound to introduce *its* architectural revolution with a play space. Other critics as well have dismissed the Saarinen hockey rink as a sheer athletic ex-

Eero Saarinen's new hockey rink at Yale breaks from all tradition and poses a challenge to academic competitors.

travaganza, even while admiring its brilliance. In appearance it has been likened variously to a Viking boat, a Paleozoic behemoth escaped from Yale's own Peabody Museum, and a stranded whale. Extravagant the rink no doubt is: all told it cost $1.4 million, a goodly sum to lay out for just another recreation in a time of so much basic academic urgency, as critics have also pointed out. But what the critics fail to appreciate is the creative potential unleashed by Yale-Harvard rivalry.

Our youthful president, A. Whitney Griswold, in a time of anxious need of new buildings to house a fast-swelling population, was in fact not particularly eager to give priority to a palace for pucksters. The heir to a Yale architectural tradition compounded also of President Grant Venetian, Early Pullman Decorated, Chicago World's Fair Roman, and excursions into Egyptian, Attic, and Moorish, he was himself a pent-up modernist in taste: but where to begin? A college president is wise to begin where the money is.

A sporting group of alumni known as the Yale Hockey Associates had told President Griswold that they had money to give for a rink; just how it might look from the outside wouldn't matter, so long as it was good to play on. Here a winning inspiration struck our president. If we must have a rink, he told them in effect, hadn't we better make it a really handsome one—and a challenge to Harvard in particular? What had Harvard built in the way of a rink? Runners were sent forth to Cambridge to photograph especially for the occasion the rival college's utilitarian shed, dated 1953 and somewhat resembling a model barn such as one might find at a Midwest state agricultural college. The opportunity was not lost upon the Hockey Associates. But if any of them thought that Dr. Griswold was about to propose something decorative in our traditional Yale sense—a Perpendicular pile like the Payne Whitney Gymnasium, say, or a brick manorial one like the Lapham field house out beside the Yale Bowl—they were due for a surprise. For at this point Griswold (Yale, '29) introduced into their

councils an astonishing model just prepared by his good friend Eero Saarinen (Yale, '34). The effect was smashing: tradition and Harvard were vanquished with one blow.

As a result, through the largesse of well-to-do and somewhat bemused skaters, Yale now finds itself with a phenomenal architectural tour de force on its grounds—a building that is not only "modern" but that goes far beyond conventional "modern" in that it leaps out from the severity and impersonality of much contemporary work to look like an individual fantasy or skylark. As if spoofing our dusty collection of architectural memorabilia, it erupts from wave-like greensward in the manner of a great bounding fish, its form given by one concrete spine arching from stem to stern and sustaining (with the aid of transverse cables) the roofing over as many as 5,000 spectators. And furthermore, with its swelling, headstrong, almost baroque lines the Saarinen rink sometimes gives the impression of mocking the current mode of cool, straight-line modern as well.

Having struck out so far, you might think that Yale could now rest awhile until the remainder of the Ivy League catches up with us. But an architectural revolution, once launched, is not easily arrested. Eero Saarinen, now a general consultant to Yale, has been commissioned to design two entire new undergraduate colleges endowed by Paul Mellon. What will *they* look like, some anxious alumni are asking, aware that they are to be sited directly between the white-faced Gothic gymnasium given by a Whitney and the red-brick Gothic Graduate School endowed by a Harkness. (They will not bound or erupt, but will be a wide-windowed cluster of contemporary brownstone purged of Gothic traces.) Moreover, the prominent plate-glass modernist Philip Johnson (most recently associated with the soaring Seagram Building on New York's Park Avenue) has been engaged to draw up a new geology laboratory for us. It won't be like the last one, which had something of the atmosphere of a donjon or keep.

Finally, still another apostle of new style, Paul Rudolph,

86

is designing a new Yale Art Center soon to rise between a mixture of the Middle Ages on one side and Chapel Street cafeterias and snuggeries on the other. "We mean to practice what we preach," declares Professor Rudolph, who is also chief of the university's architecture department. So complete is the conversion that has overtaken my alma mater in the space of only a few years that one dean recently remarked to me with an arched, superior eyebrow, "And would you believe it, down at Princeton they're still talking about designing a new building—in Gothic!" (A sheer libel, this, I learned however on checking with Princeton, which promptly sent photographs of models of a projected new dormitory quadrangle made up of neat functional boxes with not a battlement in sight.)

Shades of Ralph Adams Cram, James Gamble Rogers, and all the other academicians who dominated Yale and much of our Ivy League for so long! And shades (I thought) even of myself, who many years ago had tried to build a fire under them with a manifesto in my own campus magazine, the *Harkness Hoot*, denouncing their "frozen medievalism . . . bogus Elizabethan mansions, false and adulterous abbeys . . . twentieth-century plumbing and fifteenth-century fenestration. . . ." At the time I had written home that I might be expelled for my insurgence, and had found comfort in the fact that Frank Lloyd Wright had caused one of his students at Taliesin to leap upon a drafting table and read my philippic to the assembled company.

And where were we now? All rejecting that architectural past, evidently, and jumping collectively into the future— with a bang. And I asked myself on going back to New Haven (being a little perverse again), Was all that past really as laughable, fraudulent, and preposterous as I had thought? Over the years much of it—even some of the worst of it— had taken on a quiet glow in memory; things once silly and grotesque now seemed endearing and even handsome, if only because they (and I) had survived. Hadn't this past also become authentic in the sense that any canon of taste

Six stages of a university in search of an identity: from left, Yale's Connecticut Hall (1752), genuine, ivied Colonial; Lawrance Hall (1886), once prized for its Victorian turrets; Hewitt Quadrangle (1901), Post-office Roman; Branford Court (1920), Elizabethan; the School of Fine Arts (1928), Venetian Gothic complete with a Bridge of Sighs; Davenport College (1933), Georgian on one face and Gothic on the other, with Harkness Tower looming beyond. Missing in this sequence: the Yale Bowl—simply a bowl.

portrays the mores and feelings of its time? *Nouveau-riche* Yale in the 1920's needed to latch onto some tradition; Princeton was also true to itself then in taking on the air of a country club. How would it have been if we had redesigned wayward Yale on the basis of one fixed, over-all, immutable "modern" plan—of 1932 vintage say? Or of 1940 or thereafter? How is it with Columbia University, built according to one all-encompassing pattern that looked very modern fifty years ago—a grid of vaguely Italianate monuments? Could anything be deader today? Isn't it true, as has been said, that "Time is the chief architect of universities"— the time that gives them their changes, their characters, and their identities? And isn't it just Time that in turn lends unity to places like Yale, outrageous as its succession of outward styles may be?

Welcome to our ebullient Saarinen hockey rink, I thought: it couldn't have happened before, and it probably won't happen again. Greetings also to Mr. Saarinen with his new colleges and to Philip Johnson with his geology lab, which is sure to tell us much about the times and personality of Mr. Johnson. But greetings too—even though I say it who shouldn't—to the Powerhouse Perpendicular, girder-Gothic and false-front Colonial of our Yale past, which also were undertaken as strenuous exercises in what was thought fitting in their time: Yale wouldn't be the same without you.

The Dancing Hours, *jasper plaque by John Flaxman (1775)*

WEDGWOOD AND HIS FRIENDS

They were the most brilliant group in England, and quite possibly the most

eccentric. Some are forgotten today—but some of them changed the world

By NEIL McKENDRICK

Josiah Wedgwood was born in the Staffordshire village called Burslem in 1730. Burslem was then still rural; the country still encroached on the village, and places and properties were still spoken of in rural terms—Mill Field, Sneyd Green, and Lane End. But it was a scarred and ravaged countryside, where potters dug their clay from beside their mud and wattle hovels, hacked their coal from the surface seams of the district, and, with more thought of convenience than of beauty, dumped their waste beside their kilns. Born into the squalor and dirt of a peasant industry, Wedgwood was also born poor. The thirteenth child of a mediocre potter, his natural companions had been the sons and daughters of the local Staffordshire potters: his education, like theirs, had been sketchy and shortlived; with them, he had started work at the age of nine.

Yet in his maturity Wedgwood numbered some of the greatest men of his age amongst his friends and correspondents. His commercial success, his scientific discoveries, and his patronage of the arts had opened up a new world to him. He knew rich manufacturers, university scientists,

and famous artists. He was the Queen's Potter and possessed the entree to the fashionable society of ambassadors, aristocrats, and connoisseurs. He moved with the same ease amongst the scarlet-robed peers of the realm at Westminster as he had done with the rough potters amidst the discarded saggers and unclean streets of Burslem. He had triumphed over his origins.

Yet much as he valued his fashionable London friends his closest ties were with his friends in the Midlands, whom he had met in his youth and who formed one of the most fascinating groups in the history of the English-speaking world. At the end of the eighteenth century these active, liberal, often radical groups proliferated throughout the English provinces—at Liverpool, Warrington, Bristol, and Norwich. But the Midland group that Wedgwood knew was by far the most distinguished.

Gifted, intelligent, and odd, it was a curious mixture of brilliance and eccentricity. Brilliant in its achievements, it numbered amongst its members James Watt, the inventor of the steam engine; Joseph Priestley, the joint discoverer

WEDGWOOD

*Josiah Wedgwood, portrayed above in a medallion of his own jasper ware by William Hackwood,
became the foremost potter of eighteenth-century England. What made him famous was the
development of such desirable new wares as green glaze, Queen's Ware, and the classically
inspired jasper—to name the most celebrated. But even more important to the course of the industrial
revolution was his genius for anticipating the techniques of mass production: division of labor,
creation of demand through clever salesmanship, constant improvement of the methods of distribution,
development of cost accounting, and the application of scientific discoveries to practical problems.*

Thomas Bentley, a Liverpool merchant, became Wedgwood's partner in 1769. He took charge of the new London showroom, where his charm, urbanity, and mercantile knowledge effectively complemented Wedgwood's technical mastery.

Joseph Priestley, who discovered oxygen (although he called it "dephlogisticated air"), was introduced to Wedgwood by Bentley. Disillusioned with English politics, he eventually moved to Pennsylvania, where he died in 1804.

Like Darwin, William Withering was a successful physician with an encyclopedic range of interests: botany, dog and cattle breeding, the flute, chemistry, and the abolition of slavery.

Thomas Day made no great mark in the world beyond establishing an undisputed reputation for almost perfect eccentricity. His friends loved him and his widow died of a broken heart.

The poetess Anna Seward was called by her admirers the "Swan of Lichfield," and by the sardonic Horace Walpole a "harmonious virgin." His estimate is the one we accept today.

Erasmus Darwin was famous in his own day as a poet, talker, physician, and advocate of temperance. He drank only English wines, says a biographer, "possibly to minimize the temptation to excess." Charles was his grandson.

Benjamin Franklin was much admired by the members of the Lunar Society. Wedgwood paid tribute to the struggle of the colonists by making jasper portrait medallions of Franklin, his son, his grandson, Washington, and Lafayette.

Matthew Boulton supplied the money —and backbone—that kept the fainthearted Watt from collapsing. Without him, Watt never could have put his steam engine into general use.

The fruits of Richard Lovell Edgeworth's erratic career were four marriages, twenty-two children, many ingenious but useless inventions, and an important book on education.

In a lifetime of invention the versatile James Watt produced not only the first condensing steam engine, but—in his eighty-third year—a famous machine for copying sculpture.

of oxygen; and Matthew Boulton, the famous Birmingham manufacturer. Eccentric in its individuality, it included such figures as Erasmus Darwin, the great doctor, author, and chemist; Thomas Day, the solemn author of *The History of Sandford and Merton;* Richard Lovell Edgeworth, the lively diarist; and Anna Seward, the lovesick poetess.

They were a singular society. Famous for their science and forgotten for their literature, posterity has judged them correctly, but it has usually judged them singly. As a group they are far more interesting. For studying them together one sees through the arid wastes of commercial success and beyond the jargon of scientific discovery to the warm, human temperaments, bound together by ties which transcended religious differences and overcame political ones to become one of the most powerful agents of progress and reform that provincial England could provide.

Such a group drew others to it. Among them came William Withering, the botanist; John Baskerville, the printer; James Brindley, the engineer; George Stubbs, the artist; James Keir, the chemist; and men such as Thomas Bentley and Dr. William Small who lack the convenient label of achievement but who, by the very width of their interests, were typical of this group of friends. For thrown up by an expanding world and a changing society, they were tied together by a passionate interest in science, a lively concern for literature, and a determined search after progress and improvement. They left an astonishing heritage, astonishing not only for its importance but for its variety.

Indeed, perhaps the most remarkable aspect of this fascinating group of men was the diversity of their interests. The only comparable eighteenth-century coterie, Dr. Johnson's circle, was essentially literary, and its members—Goldsmith, Reynolds, Garrick, Boswell, Sheridan, Burke, Fox, Adam Smith, and Gibbon—had little interest in science. Wedgwood's friends were much more versatile. Drawn mainly from two separate circles—the literary Lichfield Group and the scientific Lunar Society—they had achieved an integration of the arts and the sciences which seems alien to the specialization of today. For amongst them a working knowledge of science was endemic and an active interest in the arts almost as widespread. Even Watt, the lonely, gaunt, *angst*-ridden technocrat, obsessed with science and its application, blossomed to other interests in this versatile circle. According to Sir Walter Scott, "no novel of the least celebrity escaped his perusal, and that

Joseph Wright of Derby was the first English painter to take his themes from science, and his titles were as precise as his details. This picture, exhibited in 1766, was called A Philosopher giving that Lecture on the Orrery in which a Lamp is put in the Place of the Sun *(the orrery was a popular eighteenth-century device for representing the movement of the planets in the solar system). Wright was endlessly fascinated with the problems of light, as this painting shows, but his preoccupation was as much scientific as artistic. This devotion to science naturally recommended him to Wedgwood, who became his lifelong friend and often drew on him for pottery designs and models.*

gifted man of science was . . . as shameless and obstinate a peruser of novels, as if he had been a very milliner's apprentice of eighteen."

It is characteristic of their dual interests that they thought their industrial and scientific achievements proper subjects for the arts. Nothing expresses better the experimental spirit of these Midland friends than the paintings of Wright of Derby. His canvases glow with the blast furnaces, the forges, and the fiery kilns of the Midland industries. He plundered Pliny to find a subject worthy of Wedgwood's pottery, and decorated his landscapes with the lighted windows of Arkwright's factory workers toiling through the night. Poets, too, were harnessed, to celebrate their achievements in verse. Watt's inventions, Boulton's machines, Wedgwood's canals, and Arkwright's factory were all hailed in rhyming couplets. Ponderous, deeply earnest, and redolent with pride in their own achievement, they anticipate the poems and art forms of twentieth-century Russia. Darwin, for instance, writing with more good will than effect, dwelt lovingly on the technical processes of Sir Richard Arkwright's cotton mills:

—First with nice eye emerging Naiads cull
From leathery pods the vegetable wool;
With wiry teeth *revolving cards* release
The tangled knots, and smooth the ravell'd fleece;
Next moves the *iron hand* with fingers fine,
Combs the wide card, and forms the eternal line;
Slow, with soft lips, the *whirling Can* acquires
The tender skeins, and wraps in rising spires;
With quicken'd pace *successive rollers* move,
And these retain, and those extend the *rove;*
Then fly the spoles, the rapid axles glow,
And slowly circumvolves the labouring wheel below.

It was clearly not the ideal atmosphere for poetic inspiration, but that they thought such subjects worthy of their pens illustrates the preoccupation, even of the poets amongst them, with the scientific details of industrial techniques.

The results of this preoccupation made a formidable contribution to scientific progress. It was achieved by empirical methods. They felt with Wedgwood that "Everything yields to experiment," and when Darwin defined a fool as "a man who never tried an experiment in his life" he could do so without fear of offending his friends. No subject was safe from their interest. When Wedgwood wished to find the best fertilizer and the best way to use it, he himself conducted the trials. He headed a new page in his journal for August 11, 1781: "Some Experiments for increasing the effects of a given quantity of Lime as a manure, and like wise of Dung, by dissolving them in water, and watering the land with their solutions." He proceeded carefully to record the various stages of his experiments: dung alone was tried and dung with water, dung in lumps and in solution, and finally all the available varieties of dung were tested, neatly headed "Dung of different kinds but chiefly Cow." Much

of it was written with the formality of a **corollary** to a mathematical theorem and the instructions have the absorbed care of a French recipe. For Wedgwood was absorbed and so were his friends. The same thoroughness marks all his trials: those on cobalt fill twenty closely written pages, his list of clays to be fired and tested amounts to 147 on a single page, and he fired more than 10,000 pieces of jasper before he achieved perfection.

Being confident of the powers of science and technology, Wedgwood and his friends welcomed every discovery as the harbinger of progress: Franklin's lightning conductor would usher in scientific rain-making as a substitute for the theological variety; Priestley's method of procuring pure air from the calxes of metals would introduce an age of underwater travel. Optimism came easily to them, perhaps too easily, but buoyed up by the practical successes of Brindley's bridges and canals, Wedgwood's ceramic bodies, Darwin's windmill, and Watt's steam engine, they could afford to let their imaginations soar. Some of their projects—speaking machines, air conditioning, submarines, and a flying bird powered by gunpowder or compressed air—might not bring immediate results, but they created an atmosphere of scientific enthusiasm from which blossomed the practical ideas of Priestley, Watt, and Wedgwood.

The constant interchange of scientific ideas bred abundant results: Watt's copying press sprang from Darwin's original idea, Edgeworth's carriage from a model suggested by Darwin, Wedgwood's thermometer from experiments which had interested them all.

These scientific interests found their formal expression in the Lunar Society, the famous Birmingham society which met every month on the Monday nearest the time of the full moon to enable its more distant visitors—like Wedgwood from Etruria or Darwin from Lichfield—to travel home in greater safety by its light. Held in turn in the homes of the leading spirits, it attracted scientific celebrities from the whole of Europe to air their views and answer their critics. Here, if anywhere, was the heart of this group of men, for many of Wedgwood's friends were members.

They all felt their debt to each other and they hated to miss a meeting. Even Darwin, a natural despot in personal relations, had a healthy respect for their abilities and once wrote to Boulton in 1778, "I am sorry that the infernal divinities who visit mankind with deseases, and are therefore at perpetual war with doctors, should have prevented my seeing all your great men at Soho today. Lord! what inventions, what wit, what rhetoric, metaphysical, mechanical and pyrotechnical, will be on the wing, bandied like a shuttlecock from one to another of your troop of philosophers! while . . . I, imprisoned in a postchaise, am joggl'd, and jostl'd, and bump'd and bruised along the King's highroad to make war upon a stomache-ache or a fever!"

Their individual achievements, however, were as dissimilar as their temperaments. All were talented, but not all

Josiah Wedgwood and his family (above) were painted by George Stubbs in 1780. Stubbs had been known almost exclusively as a horse painter, but Wedgwood hoped that he would prove his versatility with the family portrait (which turned out to have a strong equestrian flavor anyway). The eldest daughter, Susannah, became the mother of Charles Darwin. Tom (on pony, left) was an early photographer.

Wedgwood's famed Etruria works (below) were opened in 1769 and named for the ancient Etruscan potters who inspired some of his early ornamental ware. The historic old factory was in continuous use until 1950, when it was finally abandoned for the new plant at Barlaston. By that time, as a result of coal-mining operations in the neighborhood, the level of the ground floor had sunk below the canal.

were effective. Worldly success came only to those with stamina and endurance: Watt, Wedgwood, and Boulton achieved their success only by resolute application and unremitting toil. Fully integrated characters, they had a fixed aim in life and they achieved it. They disciplined their personalities. The others in this circle were more indulgent, they allowed their temperaments free rein. Darwin and Priestley, for instance, refused to compromise with their natures for the sake of their careers. Priestley's passion for polemics threatened to disrupt his career, and his blind faith in an obsolete theory of combustion jeopardized his discovery of oxygen. Yet he always followed his natural impulse: he suffered exile rather than cloak his political beliefs and missed the significance of his greatest discovery rather than alter his opinions. Darwin, too, lived his life on his own terms: he stammered out his views whatever the company and indulged his "love of Venus" despite his medical profession. The genius of Darwin and Priestley was such that their reputations have survived their obsessions, unlike those of the less gifted members of this group.

Bentley preferred to exercise his charm rather than to regiment his gifts; Anna Seward chose to warm herself before the cozy admiration of her friends and to preoccupy herself with their lives rather than to heed the London critics and acknowledge her limitations; Thomas Day spent his time in a mad pursuit of his idea of the perfect female relationship and strangled his literary talent in the undergrowth of his quaint opinions; whilst Edgeworth's pursuit of the sex as a whole and his dilettante attitude to his work choked any serious contribution to science.

Erasmus Darwin, "that large mass of genius and sarcasm" as Anna Seward called him, was the strange and startling patriarch of this circle of friends. Ugly, fat, lame, clumsy, and stammering, Darwin moved through the Midlands fathering two bastard daughters and shocking his listeners by his openly expressed atheism, yet his reputation survived undiminished, his influence unrivaled. By sheer weight of character he was able to flout the normal conventions—even to the extent of unprofessional conduct, making love as a widower of fifty to an attractive young married patient and marrying her on her husband's timely death in the face of the competition of "half the wealthy youth of Derbyshire."

His huge shambling figure was a landmark in intellectual society, and in Lichfield he was regarded with awe. An able doctor and a competent scientist, his formidable personality proved an admirable substitute for literary talent. Once

his poetry stood alone, divorced from the intimidating aura of Darwin himself, it was quickly forgotten.

Like his friends, Darwin was fascinated by experiment and scientific techniques: as a doctor he was always ready to try new methods, and dramatic cures swelled his reputation; whilst his public dissections of the corpses of freshly hanged criminals added a colorful touch to his name. The gadgets that preoccupied his mind and filled his home furthered the impression of mysterious skill. A casual order for some hot coals through his speaking tube, for instance, once sent a visitor, who was waiting in the kitchen and unused to such a device, running terrified from the house convinced that it was haunted. His carriage was equally unusual. It was equipped with all the conveniences of a maisonette. To satisfy his huge bulk he carried on his left a hamper of fruits and sweetmeats, cream and sugar. In front of him was a place for his knife, fork, and spoon, and for writing paper and pencils. On the other side was a well-stocked bookcase rising from the floor to the window. Above him was a skylight and shade with which he could regulate the light for reading. Whilst he went about his calls he read, wrote, and ate, and the carriage became so well known that he once got a letter addressed to "Dr. Darwin, Upon the Road."

Thomas Day was even stranger. From the first he rejected the habits and customs of what he regarded as a "perverse and foolish world": his dress rarely conformed to the accepted standards of society; his opinions never did. In an age of masculine elegance he dressed like a savage. In his search for a wife he displayed even odder standards. Unable to find the paragon he required amongst mature women, he decided that the only logical plan was to raise his own wife, or rather to mold one to fit his own requirements. Buoyed up with new enthusiasm, he picked two pretty twelve-year-olds from foundling hospitals and christened them Sabrina and Lucretia. He conducted the experiment in duplicate, with no bigamous intent, merely as a security measure offering double the possibility of success. But even in duplicate his plan was doomed.

One of Wedgwood's best-known medallions (above) was commissioned from William Hackwood in 1768 and became the seal of the Slave Emancipation Society. At right is a self-portrait of George Stubbs on horseback. Stubbs was a student of anatomy, and the authority with which the horse is painted reflects his four years of dissecting them on a lonely farm.

CONTINUED ON PAGE 128

By WILLIAM K. ZINSSER

Is it true what the movies say about...

In the year 1958, when Good Queen Bardot ruled the movie world and it was hardly worth exposing a film unless the star was exposing her body, a curious bit of surgery took place. An American movie exhibitor received from Sweden a picture that he had agreed to release in this country. To his horror, it contained no nude bathing scenes.

There was only one thing to do, and he did it. He found some nude bathing scenes elsewhere and spliced them into the movie at points where the action seemed to lag. Thus he gave his film what the trade calls a "hypo." For it is a law of economics that a movie prospers in direct ratio to the number of maids who disrobe while the plot runs its course.

This probably was not the exhibitor's motive. I think he was merely trying to achieve an authentic portrait of Sweden, which this movie obviously was not. For anyone who has seen a Swedish film knows that nude bathing is common, perhaps even compulsory, in that land. The ones that I have watched were all bleak and Gothic tales, but in each case I was pleasantly surprised to see the young lovers slip out of their civvies and into a silvery lake as casually as if they were stopping for a malted at the corner drugstore.

Why the travel agents don't publicize this aspect of Scandinavian life I can't imagine. They never get through to me, somehow, with all their talk of fiords and reindeer herds, but I'd gladly stop off for a few days in any country where the girls look like *September Morn*. I can only conclude that, since travel agents don't overlook even the tiniest "point of interest"—no matter how uninteresting it really is—nude bathing is actually not a Swedish custom, and the nation's movies do not reflect the nation's habits.

But then, does any country create a true portrait of itself on film? In France, if its movies are any index, no husband would dream of going home to his own bedroom at night. A far stronger instinct takes him to the boudoir of his mistress, a worldly beauty of the type that composes half the population of Paris. If he did go home that would be the last place to find his wife, for she steals off every afternoon to comfort some handsome young devil like Gérard Philipe.

Of course I may have the wrong impression of France,

The Lavender Hill Mob

the British

La Parisienne

the French

One Summer of Happiness

the Swedes

too. Conceivably there are millions of husbands and wives who like each other. It may be possible to walk the full length of the Riviera and not see a Brigitte Bardot changing from her street clothes into a bandanna, or even a Band-Aid. But the world sees France through her movies, and in this mirror a land of eternal revels is reflected.

If you are not looking for pagan pleasures the place to go is Britain. Now there's a country with charm. Most of the men are whimsical chaps like Alec Guinness, who dabble in robbery and homicide but do it in such a funny way that you can't help liking them, or antic villagers of the kind that hid the whisky in *Tight Little Island*, or jolly manor lords who talk of cricket so amusingly that they sound like Noel Coward or Oscar Wilde.

The remaining Britons fall into a second—and last—category. They are the officers who go off to their fate with a nonchalance that only centuries of breeding can mold: "I shouldn't wait up if I were you, Pam—Jerry may keep us busy for a few days." Pam herself, who guesses the truth—that her husband is going to swim underwater into Hamburg with a bomb in his teeth—smiles bravely and says, "Cheerio, Nigel. Don't fret about me and little Robin—we'll all be together for the week end, you'll see."

I began crying over this kind of thing in *Cavalcade* and haven't stopped yet. Rarely do I see an English picture in which the stiff upper lip turns soft, in which the British Isles are revealed to have some seamy citizens, too. Most of these are Cockneys, who speak a language seldom identifiable as the mother tongue. This makes the movie sound so alien, a product of some country like Bulgaria, that it leaves unsullied my vision of England as the ideal blend of droll spirit and noble heart.

Italy, in the years after the war, came closest to capturing the truth about itself on film. Several directors, notably Roberto Rossellini and Vittorio De Sica, made films of heartbreaking honesty, such as *Open City*, *Paisan*, *Shoe Shine*, and *The Bicycle Thief*. They didn't build sets; they simply took their cameras into the streets, and for stars they chose ordinary people who looked right for the role. The resulting films were a poignant study of men, women, and children caught in the tides of war and the rubble of peace.

But these movies were too true for the Italians, who shunned them at the box office, not caring to be reminded of what they already knew. Italy's movie industry quickly began making movies that the people really wanted to see. They were breezy fables that didn't represent the country but did gratify the popular taste for escapist fare.

Through these films such ripe lasses as Gina Lollobrigida, Silvana Mangano, and Sophia Loren rose to fame and fortune. De Sica went back to acting, his original métier, and hasn't done much directing since. When he does, as in *Gold of Naples*, the picture has his customary stamp of humor and humanity, but such pictures emerge rarely from Italy now. Only one other director seems to have De Sica's art and compassion, and that is Federico Fellini. In *Vitelloni*, *La Strada*, and *Cabiria* he indicates a growth that could make him the giant in his field.

Many countries, though they fail to reflect their present, do a glorious job of etching their past on film. The past is conveniently vague and can be decked in all the robes of chivalry and romance. The American western, for example, endows its sheriffs and cowboys with the most sterling virtues, and even the goodhearted prostitute who runs the Deadwood Saloon is, beneath her shabby calling, so goodhearted that she seems little short of saintly.

Japan is the most brilliant custodian of its own past. This makes sense, for today's Tokyo looks like today's Chicago, its people wear suits of Yankee cut, and the MacArthur dynasty has left its impress on the nation far more than the dynasty of Hirohito. The present is drab, the past ornate. Hence the movies which Japan sends to the outside world reconstruct the feudal age; a time of proud barons, pretty princesses, and a samurai code that enabled brave men to win honor with the sword. They are movies that indulge the exotic and our craving for fairy tales.

This age has vanished, of course, and yet in a way it represents the best and most enduring Japan of all—the world that is preserved for us in Japanese art. What bewitches us in a Japanese screen or print is its unerring color and design. When movies came along the Japanese used the

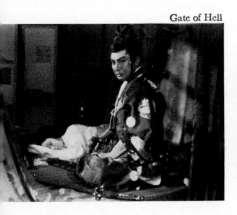
Gate of Hell

the Japanese

The Bicycle Thief

the Italians

Pather Panchali

the Indians

. . . and the Americans ▶

medium with the same fastidious eye, and so it is that their best films are like a classical print come to life. *Gate of Hell*, for instance, was literally breath-taking from beginning to end. Many people remember it as their most vivid impression of Japan. It didn't represent the country as you would see it today. But it did represent the Japanese nature.

In the case of the United States the problem is peculiarly thorny. There is no corner of the globe that Hollywood's charades do not reach. In fact, now that the movie audience in this country is dwindling, our industry earns 45 per cent of its money from foreign box offices. Obviously the world's image of us is shaped almost entirely by our movies, and as many commentators have pointed out, this is not our best image, or even a fair one. We continue to breed clichés about our country that are just as rigid, and false, as the French cliché of the philandering mate or the British cliché of the funny bank robber.

What do we know of the Midwest through our movies? Very little. Those flat colonies beyond the Mississippi loom as one immense college campus, where the peppy cheerleader and the jovial halfback drop their megaphone and football in the final reel to elope, thus carrying on the breed. Imagine my surprise, on going to Iowa a few years ago, to find that the region also has cities and farms, and that the people have attitudes quite different from people in the east and the west.

But not until *Picnic* in 1956 did I see a movie that captured the feeling of the farm belt. Joshua Logan made the film in a Kansas town so plain that it looked like a thousand other American towns. He photographed its homely frame houses with their porch swings, cluttered parlors, and crab-grass lawns that creep out over the sidewalk. He shot the brick high school and the sluggish river in the middle of town and the freight yards at the edge. Beyond the town he framed some huge grain elevators against a pale blue sky

and a flat landscape of wheat that stretched out to the horizon. He even recorded the sounds of summer, like the banging of the back screen door.

Thus he told the movie-goer that a small Midwest town is a tiny unit in the middle of nothing, that its interests are indrawn and its currents of gossip strong, and that those who break away to the outside world do so only by breaking off their entire past. This is a central fact of life in the Midwest—it affects those who stay as much as those who go—and it is a deeply dramatic fact. It is a theme dear to American literature, but *Picnic* marked its rare treatment on the screen. As the movie reached its climax at a Labor Day picnic—a supremely American event with its wheezy musicians on a flag-draped bandstand, its male quartets and shrill sopranos, its pie-eating contests, three-legged races, watermelons, and lost babies—various characters also reached a turning point in their lives, and by then we were in a position to understand the factors of environment that shaped their decisions.

Here is an American vein that Hollywood has hardly tapped. Nor do I know much, as a movie fan, about the Southwest and the Northwest—*Giant* and *Bus Stop* were only a beginning—and I know almost nothing about the booming state of California.

And what about Hollywood's version of the South? The pre-Civil War days fall into a picturesque pattern long fixed by national folklore. Kindly old Massa rules the plantation not with a whip but a swizzle stick, while white bewhiskered Negroes bring him juleps and sing spirituals in the cotton fields, as their mammies did before them, and Miss Eulabelle holds court to the local fops. Fair enough, I suppose—this kind of thing is by now as stylized as the western.

But the modern South is a different matter. Its most celebrated bards are William Faulkner, Erskine Caldwell, and Tennessee Williams. From most of the recent movies based on their works you would assume the South to be inhabited solely by lynchers, barn burners, rapists, hillbillies, sex-starved blondes, vengeful old patriarchs, and idiot sons.

Most were good movies. But none of them touched the human issues that make the South today one of America's most dramatic regions. It is an area afflicted by hatreds so old and inbred that they can be exorcised only in pain, an area where the bigots are far outnumbered by gentle citizens who sincerely want to solve the problem that darkens their lives, but don't know how. In this situation there are dozens of movies that would touch the heart.

Sometimes a good portrait of America comes from a surprising origin. Who would have thought that *Peyton Place* would be such a film? As everybody knows, the novel had little patience with its characters once they were out

Amid many Hollywood distortions of Midwestern life, says Mr. Zinser, the film Picnic *stands out for its truthful look at a small town.*

of bed and dressed, but it did have a New England setting, and from this threshold Hollywood made a movie that had an authentic American flavor.

Several of its plots were quite racy, but in general it dealt with the ordinary things that happen to people during the cycle of a New England year. First of all, it had pictorial beauty. Director Mark Robson realized that the town itself was one of the movie's stars, and he let his camera wander over its features—old white churches and elm-lined streets, clapboard houses and brick mills—so that, as the seasons changed and spring released the ground from snow and yielded in turn to drowsy summer and garish fall, the movie-goer had a feeling for the rhythm of the community.

Against this background Robson shot some of the rituals that are part of the growing-up process in towns all over America. The movie also recognized that life has subtle seasons of its own, such as the summer after high-school graduation, a summer that is like no other, bridging the world of child and adult. In these details *Peyton Place* touched some of America's deepest roots, for it sought plain truths and was satisfied to set them down plainly.

New York has been the subject of many movies, most of them inflated far beyond reality. They paint New Yorkers as a suave and wealthy breed, oscillating between penthouse and Stork Club, their girls a race of goddesses swathed in money and mink. It is a temptation hard to resist, for Manhattan has glamour, and if there's one thing that Hollywood wants to put on the screen it's glamour. That's what movies are for—to some extent. But recently quite a few films have also dealt with the real New Yorkers, the millions who do not have wealth or beauty or glamour, who are acutely lonely though they dwell in the most populous city on earth.

Marty, of course, is the classic example of the movie that glimpsed the heartache of urban man. Tenderly and with humor it told the story of a pudgy Bronx butcher and a shy girl, who had given up hope that love would ever find them. The movie looked real because it was filmed against real neon store fronts, subway stations, and other such local landmarks. But that was not the secret of its spell.

Its truth lay in the honesty of its dialogue and the purity of its vision, for never once did it make its characters do something unnatural for the sake of dramatic effect or cheapen their affair with a joke that didn't belong. Their search for love, and their wonder at discovering it, were touching because in this search everyone in the audience saw something of himself.

Other recent movies of New York that had this same honesty were *A Hatful of Rain*, *Edge of the City*, *Sweet Smell of Success*, and *Blackboard Jungle*. But these films were somewhat unsavory and they brought into the open a problem that

Peyton Place, *as adapted for Hollywood from the widely debated novel, won critics' praise as an honest portrayal of Americans today.*

has long vexed Americans who fear for our reputation. *Blackboard Jungle*—to take the most notorious—was a taut drama of violence in a New York high school, partly touched off by racial tensions. It did not reflect all American high schools and actually damaged our good name abroad.

Still, no believer in the American freedoms would say that the movie should not have been made, or that the government should forbid its sale outside this country. Censorship is the death of art. Nor can any censor foresee exactly what impression a movie will make, as *The Grapes of Wrath* once proved to the Kremlin's surprise. The Russians exhibited the picture widely, intending to illustrate the sordid nature of life in the United States. But the fact that the Okies had a car, decrepit as it was, put them one up on the Soviet movie-goers, and the film was withdrawn.

Hollywood is under no obligation to paint America in rosy colors. But the industry is financially obliged to save its skin, and all the tricks that science can devise—wide screens, stereophonic sound, Smell-o-vision, and subliminal persuaders—will not bring Americans back into the movie house if the story is bad. There is a basic instinct about this. It is no accident that *Our Town* is America's most durable drama. Year after year Thornton Wilder's play is performed in hundreds of schools, colleges, and theatrical societies. It speaks to young and old, rich and poor. It touches every man's experience because it deals in universal truths.

Such stories abound in our land and Hollywood has not begun to tell them. Every town in America is "Our Town" if the moviemakers approach it from the right direction—and know what to do when they get there.

William K. Zinsser served notably as movie critic of the New York Herald Tribune. *Now an editorial writer he still has firm opinions about Moviedom. In the January* HORIZON *he wrote "The Tyranny of the Teens."*

Twelve thousand fragments

in an Emperor's sculpture gallery

make a jigsaw puzzle for archaeologists

THE CAVE OF TIBERIUS

By ROBERT EMMETT GINNA

But after the loss of his two sons, of whom Germanicus died in Syria and Drusus at Rome, he withdrew into Campania; at which time opinion and conversation were widespread that he would never return and would soon die. And both turned out to be nearly true. For, indeed, he never returned to Rome, and a few days after leaving it, when he was at a villa of his called "The Cave" near Terracina, during supper a number of stones fell from above killing many of the guests and attendants, but he almost miraculously escaped.

> The Twelve Caesars, *by G. Suetonius Tranquillus,* Tiberius, *Book III, Chapter XXXIX*

In the late summer of 1957 a gang of men labored beneath the grilling sun, building a road along the Tyrrhenian Sea between Terracina and Gaeta. Just south of Sperlonga, 126 kilometers below Rome, the new highway intersects an ancient Roman way known as the Via Flacca.

At this juncture the Via Flacca cuts through a promontory, on the south side of which are the extensive remains of a Roman villa. While the road gang was engaged in the area, this villa was being excavated by archaeologists working under the direction of Professor Giulio Jacopi, Superintendent of Antiquities for Rome and the Province of Latina.

The coastal region from Anzio to Baia is studded with the vestiges of villas occupied in Roman times by prominent citizens, who found them refuges from the pressures of public life and the strain of almost continual warfare. Here such men as Cicero, Hortensius, and Lucullus took their

Two of the exquisite treasures found in the Cave of Tiberius are the life-sized head of a bearded man (opposite) presumed to be Odysseus, and the slightly larger than life size Ganymedes (right).

ease amid gardens embellished with statuary and fountains.

Besides these evidences of Roman grandeur, this coast holds many associations, real and legendary, to stir the blood of the archaeologist. Hannibal campaigned here during the Second Punic War. Along this shore Odysseus was supposed to have voyaged, losing his men to the cannibalistic Laestrygones and shunning the Sirens' song.

The town of Sperlonga, mounted on high cliffs, juts out from the coast. Strabo noted that in these cliffs were caverns "affording cool retreats, attached to the Roman villas built around." Just on the north side of the promontory, where the excavation of the villa was in progress, one such cavern debouched onto the sea. Local legend attributed to it some association with the *imperatóre misántropo*. To the archaeologists this recalled the passages of Suetonius—and Tacitus as well—concerning the incident of the Emperor Tiberius narrowly escaping death in such a cave.

With the crew on this stretch of highway was an engineer, Erno Bellante, who was also an amateur archaeologist. As he was in touch with the professional archaeologists already working on the cape, he offered to undertake an exploration of the grotto that could be seen in the cliff face above a field of artichokes. Bellante started on September 6. Almost immediately he reported finding many sculptural fragments. Professor Jacopi hurried to assume direction of the operation. In a short time it was clear that an archaeological find of the first magnitude had been made: an extensive complex of buildings bordering the several-chambered grotto, which itself contained quantities of broken statuary of high quality. Both the building complex and sculptural remains appeared to span a period of four or five centuries.

With every scoop of the shovel the archaeologists became more certain that they had located what had once been the gallery of a collector of wealth and refinement. And the evidence of ancient authors, checked against their findings, left little doubt in their minds that one master of the grotto had been none other than Tiberius Caesar.

Within three weeks of the discovery further findings touched off a series of controversies ranging from near revolution at Sperlonga to upheaval in scholastic citadels. Archaeological strikes are made regularly in Italy, but this one acquired prominence in newspapers the world over. What brought this about was the finding of an inscription in several fragments which, when pieced together, showed the first five letters of the name Hagesandros, the entire name Athenodoros, and the last five letters of the name Polydoros.

Pliny had written in his *Natural History*, "Out of one block of stone the consummate artists, Hagesandros, Polydoros, and Athenodoros of Rhodes made, after careful planning, Laocoön, his sons, and the snakes marvelously entwined about them." Laocoön was the priest of Thymbraean Apollo who had warned the Trojans against admitting the wooden horse of the Greeks to their city and had been ignored. He had angered Apollo by begetting children, despite his vow of celibacy, and doing so within the temple precinct. As punishment, and as warning of Troy's doom, Apollo sent two serpents to crush Laocoön and his two sons.

On January 14, 1506, the Laocoön sculpture, lost since antiquity, was unearthed from the ruins of the house of the Emperor Titus on the Esquiline hill in Rome, where Pliny had said that it stood. Since its discovery it has been a treasure of the Vatican collection. The distinguished scholar Margarete Bieber has called the Vatican Laocoön "Probably the most widely discussed work of sculpture which we possess from antiquity." Poets extolled the sculpture, and it was studied by Michelangelo, whose work was influenced by its muscular passion. Lessing and Goethe wrote essays about it. William Blake made a print after it, in which he transformed Laocoön and his two sons into "Jehovah and his two sons, Satan and Adam, as they were copied from the Cherubim of Solomon's Temple by three Rhodians and applied to National Fact or History of Ilium."

The magnificent statue in the Vatican was generally accepted as the original work of the Rhodian masters. Now this inscription was found at Sperlonga bearing the names of the acknowledged authors of the Laocoön. And near the inscription were found pieces of statuary which clearly had belonged to figures in dynamic attitudes. Two life-sized torsos were recovered and a heroic leg which alone stands seven feet high. Had the original Laocoön been found? The Vatican statue bore no signature, although few classical originals did. Could the Vatican work be merely a copy, as was so common in imperial Rome? This sort of speculation gained international attention for the discoveries at Sperlonga and started eager disputes among the scholars. Nor was the notoriety of the discovery lost on the citizens of Sperlonga. Foreseeing a lucrative tourist trade, they threatened to blow up the grotto and all it contained if a single fragment were removed from it. To implement their threat they dug a trench about the place. The archaeologists sought and received police protection.

The excavations already completed and those still under way have revealed in and about the grotto an elaborate design of pools and waterworks executed with impressive workmanship. These were enhanced by a number of sculptural groups and numerous individual figures in marble, most of splendid quality, and some which are manifestly the works of notable Hellenistic schools. The plan appears to have been progressively enlarged, displaying various phases and styles of construction and decoration that make it possible to fix its duration over four or five centuries commencing toward the end of the Republic in the first century B.C. Within the grotto several smaller chambers open from the main one. Around these chambers are numerous niche seats, some hewn from the rock, others constructed in masonry. The central chamber is almost entirely occupied by

Two statues in the Vatican Museum which assume interest because of related finds at Sperlonga are Ganymedes seized by the eagle and the Laocoön group showing the priest and his two sons being crushed by serpents. The Laocoön, found in Rome in 1506, has long been accepted as the original from Rhodes.

Seen from the Cave of Tiberius, across the great circular pool, the town of Sperlonga forms the background, perched on its headland above the Tyrrhenian Sea. The base in the center of the pool undoubtedly supported a sculptural group. The high scaffold will support the "Laocoön" in reconstruction.

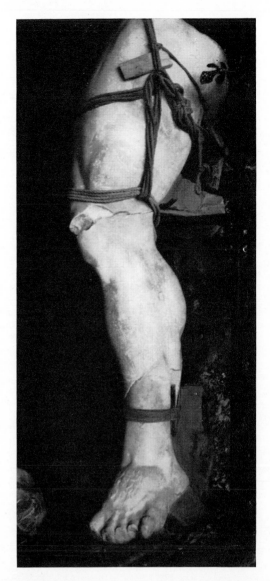

The heroic puzzle confronting the archaeologists is exemplified by the maze of statuary in the photograph below. Several hundred fragments of the 12,000 found to date are piled in a small antechamber adjoining the central chamber of the grotto. In this collection are the two magnificent torsos shown at left and right above.

The leg at left is the principal component of the statue which Archaeologist Jacopi believes may be the Laocoön. It stands about seven feet high. The two life-sized torsos found near it have been thought to represent the sons of the Trojan priest. But their anatomy is more mature than that of the two youths of the Vatican statue.

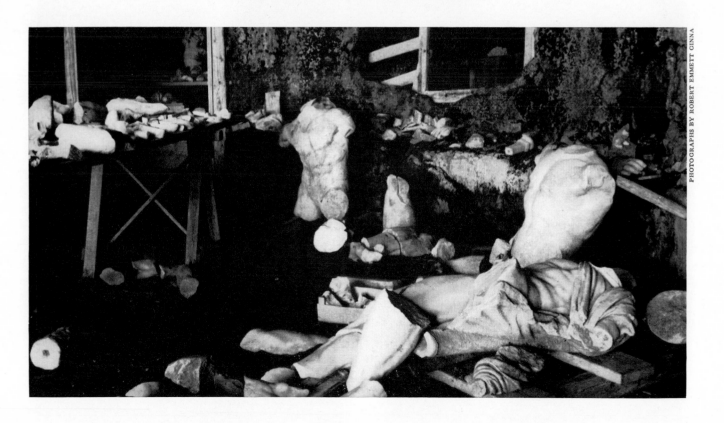

a spring-fed, fresh-water pool about seventy-five feet in diameter. In front of the grotto is an arrangement of rectangular pools, fed by the one within the grotto. The walls of the chambers show traces of polychromy and stucco work as well as the vitreous mosaics and inlaid sea shells with which they were formerly adorned. Remnants of these decorations can be seen over the mouth of the grotto.

On the terrace before and to the side of the principal cave (for several other, smaller caves open from the precipitous hillside) are the extensive foundations of buildings dating for the most part from the first century A.D. Some sections of wall survive and from these and from the ground plentiful fragments of mural decoration have been recovered. These are largely in the so-called third and fourth Pompeian styles of the first century A.D. and consist of delicately rendered imaginary architectural constructions amid which characters from mythology are painted.

From the several layers of brick and plaster (some within one another, others alongside or atop one another), it is apparent that the buildings date from the first century B.C. into the third century A.D.; the earliest style being the loose stone and mortar work termed *opus incertum*, the latest being the elaborate brickwork termed the "cortina" style. The scale of the construction and its lavish decorative treatment lend support to the theory that this had indeed been the pleasure dome of a Roman emperor.

Tiberius, second emperor of Rome, acceded to the role after the death of Augustus in A.D. 14. He ruled over the Empire until his own death at seventy-nine years of age in A.D. 37. Tiberius Caesar has not fared well in history. He is generally presented as a paradox, something of a double personality: the one that of a sober soldier-statesman; the other a depraved tyrant, treacherous and cunning to an extreme. Until the end of the last century the black side of this portrait was predominant. This has in large measure been due to the accounts of his reign by Suetonius and Tacitus, who both flourished some years after it. Suetonius in particular related with lurid detail the violent and debauched deeds attributed to the aged Emperor in the last years of his life, which he passed on Capri. Yet Plutarch, who abhorred vice, writing at the same time as Tacitus, exhibits nothing but respect for Tiberius. Today, he is the subject of considerable re-evaluation by historians.

In Book IV of his *Annals* Tacitus wrote that in his old age Tiberius left Rome for Campania (the province stretching south from Rome to Sorrento between the mountains and the sea). Tacitus averred that the Emperor betook himself from the capital in order to pursue his debaucheries less observed and said that Tiberius had done the same thing as a younger man when he chose to dwell on the island of Rhodes. He added that the Emperor was ashamed of his tall, stooped figure, balding head, and blotchy face.

Wrote Tacitus: "About this time a danger confronted Tiberius which added strength to idle rumors and gave him cause for increased confidence in the loyalty and staunchness of Sejanus. They were dining in a villa called Spelunca, situated between the sea at Amyclae and the hills of Fundi, inside a natural cave. All of a sudden, the mouth of the cave fell in, stones poured down and crushed some of the attendants; a general panic ensued, and the guests fled. Throwing himself above the Emperor's person on his knees, hands and face, Sejanus warded off the falling stones, and in this position he was found by the soldiers who came to the rescue."

The account by Tacitus locates the grotto. Sperlonga is merely a corruption of the Latin *spelunca*, meaning cave. The wonder is that the grotto was never explored, considering the legend attached to it and the ancient descriptions. The agreement of Suetonius and Tacitus on the falling stones at first inclined the archaeologists to the idea that the shattered statuary was the result of the disaster during Tiberius' banquet. This theory was discarded when closer observation indicated that the marbles seemed to have been fractured by the blows of hammers. Moreover, there is no sign of the vault ever having collapsed to any serious degree.

Both the architectural styles and certain sculptural remains demonstrate that the grotto was occupied for more than a century after Tiberius' reign ended. A sculptural portrait of an unidentified man has been recovered, executed in a manner characteristic of the third century A.D. One of the most interesting discoveries at the site has been the excavation of a small chapel with a vaulted roof, cut out of the steep hill alongside the principal cave. It had been paved with a plain white mosaic floor and decorated with stuccowork, traces of which remain. That this was a site of Christian worship is evident from a small cross and the words AVE CRVX SANCTA incised in the wall.

This chapel may provide a clue to the mystery of the destruction of the sumptuous statuary which once graced the grotto. Possibly when the site became a place of Christian devotions the sculptural images of pagan mythology were destroyed by religious zealots. A further clue was the location of a large oven or kiln in the hillside. As can be seen in such prints as Piranesi's, the firing of marble in kilns to obtain lime was a common practice, which accounted for the disappearance of numberless Roman works. Much of imperial Rome was reduced to ash, not by the barbarians but by the Romans during the Middle Ages and later.

In attempting to identify the grotto as the resort of Tiberius, archaeologists have noticed some possibly significant facts. Certain sculptural groups at Sperlonga are already known through versions attributed to sculptors who lived on the island of Rhodes. Moreover, other fragments not yet positively identified exhibit treatment which is characteristically Rhodian. What gives these facts significance is that Tiberius spent seven years of his life on Rhodes.

When he was thirty-five years old, after a notable career as an army commander and after serving as governor of Gaul, quaestor, and consul, Tiberius was invested with the

CONTINUED ON PAGE 122

108

The Gallic Laughter of
ANDRE FRANCOIS

An exuberant satirist and prankster, this unpredictable

Frenchman combines witty insight with the clarity

of high art. So writes a noted American colleague

By BEN SHAHN

Whether art is good art or bad art has nothing to do with whether it is satiric or solemn. I suppose that the soberer commentators of every age have tried to exclude the humorous from their immediate purview. But their failure to do so is attested by a long and great line of works which, if they have been thrown out the front door of art, have returned by the back to sit enthroned today among the noblest works. Who would exile from art the Greek satyr, the monsters of the Byzantine columns with their curious preoccupations, the gargoyles of Notre Dame, the subhuman and ultrahuman characters of Bosch and Bruegel? Who would seek to dismiss Callot or Daumier or Hogarth from art?

Today there are a few satirical artists whose work is to be considered good and very serious art—serious if not sober. I think of Robert Osborn and Saul Steinberg here in the United States, of Ronald Searle in England, of Maccari in Italy, and of André François in France. And of course there is the immortal George Grosz whose work struck the prewar world of the twenties with such impact and revelation. The drawings of these men will assuredly live as have those of Callot and Daumier.

I am not as a rule a very avid meeter of people. I like best the ones I find haphazardly, the casual acquaintances, the indigenous population of any country I happen to visit. But I must confess that a few years ago when I returned to France I looked forward to meeting André François. It was not just that I liked his drawings, but rather that I knew through his drawings that I would like him. And so I did, and do.

He is not unlike his drawings, François. Note the one reproduced on page 119 of the mighty façade of Notre Dame and the two little autos which happened to meet head-on in the wide plaza. On our arrival in Paris François called me from his home in Grisy-les-Plâtres and warmly invited my wife and me to come for a visit; he would call for us by car the following morning—I think that was a Saturday evening. At about noon on Sunday he called

109

again, very apologetic, very regretful; his automobile had a frozen motor and there would be some delay. He called a little later, however, to say that he had a friend who would be pleased to drive us; he would probably arrive within the hour. Within the hour François called again. He was so sorry for our inconvenience; his friend's car had been stolen but he thought that he might be able to find another friend with a car. Soon he called again: everything was fine at last; his friend had simply misplaced his car. Now he had found it and was probably already waiting for us below. By the time we actually met we had shared enough crises already to be familiar friends.

A week or so later my wife and I had just unsuccessfully tried to call François when we came upon him sitting with a friend in front of a café. He sprang to his feet and with his usual charm and courtesy introduced his friend, a M. Ronancière. He excused himself saying that he would take M. Ronancière to a taxi and return immediately. Within a few minutes I noticed a disturbance and looked up to see André and his friend rushing back across the street toward us in defiance of the harebrained Paris traffic.

They came back to us. André's friend exclaimed, "You're Ben Shahn! André mumbles so that I didn't catch your name." He pumped my hand.

I thanked the gentleman, who appeared to be British, and we said goodbye again. When André returned I said to him, "What a nice fellow that seemed to be. Actually I couldn't say so before him, but I didn't catch his name either."

"Oh that," said André, "was M'sieu Ronald Searle of London."

"Go get him back!" I shouted. André went but Searle had left.

Everything was mended however when, on the following day, we all met for lunch, André promising to take us afterward to a highly interesting auction of lost and stolen articles picked up by the Paris police. We somehow failed to find the auction, but wound up in a dungeon below the Hôtel de Ville, alongside the guillotine that had beheaded Marie Antoinette.

Such small incidents are but emanations of the naturally lugubrious soul that is concealed beneath the gracious, modest, and decorous exterior of François.

The soul itself is at its best in his drawings; it seems most at home there. With most of us the soul is a deeply buried affair, making its appearance now and then in strange and unaccountable acts and images. The life of an artist, perhaps of any so-called creative person, might be described as a long self-denuding process—a sort of search to discover just who exactly he is, what he wants, what he really likes and is like. Whenever he finally succeeds in unwrapping all the swaddling clothes with which he was wrapped at birth (if he ever does succeed) then, theoretically, he ought to know what to paint or write, and just how to go about it.

Of course, if he doesn't care to accept what he finds, or to risk so much exposure, he may go through life dressed like someone else—a common enough solution. With François one feels that he was perhaps born with this sort of complete understanding of himself; that he must have been long acquainted with whatever foibles were his and perfectly resigned to living with them and even elaborating on them a little. This is not to suggest that he has more imperfections than the rest of us, only that he enjoys them more.

What are imperfections anyway, except departures from the norm? Really to appreciate imperfection, one should perhaps examine its opposite: perfection—perfection in drawing, for instance.

One might say that perfection in drawing, if it ever came about, would be the complete removal of the personal element in an artist's work—naturally the personal weaknesses. Thus, when a drawing finally reached what could be called perfection, it would be about as impersonal as drawing could be. On the other side of the scale one might say that the ultimate in imperfection would be the most completely personal statement an artist could make. François' drawings are, in an academic sense, about the ultimate in imperfection, and they are by all odds the most completely, wholly personal drawings that one sees today.

I must hasten to explain that by "imperfection" I do not imply weak or poor drawing. On the contrary, François

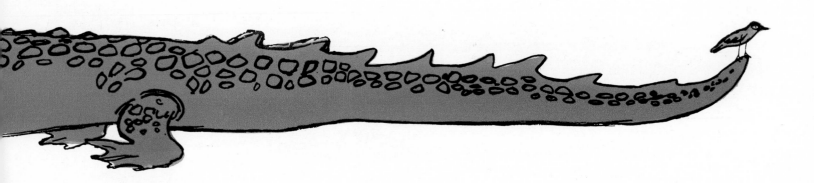

ILLUSTRATION FROM *Crocodile Tears*

Cartoonist, illustrator, and accomplished painter, François invests all his work and surroundings with a quality of surprise. Visitors to his house outside Paris can never be absolutely sure whether the objects they see before them are real or sheer, painted fabrication. Here the bull's-eye window and its recess exist in reality, but the bookshelves, books, telephone, and assorted bric-a-brac are all trompe-l'œil deception. And the dog peeking out of the cupboard is simply a portrait of the family pet.

stands among the best as a master of expressive drawing. He knows the spirit and the mood that he wants to impart and goes to it directly. You might say that he is innocent of pedantry and academism. He thinks only of what he wants to say and says it.

I had first seen François' drawings in *Punch*, and followed them with great pleasure and interest. Then his book *The Tattooed Sailor* appeared; that was an unparalleled delight for its outright wit and its lugubrious undertone of the ponderous strivings of the human animal to be divine, but most of all for its straight and great drawing. Thus, when I met the artist and learned that he is also an earnest painter, I was almost afraid to see his painting for fear it would be less direct than his drawing.

That's an inner affliction I carry around with me— the dread that people's more serious work will be less serious than their less serious work. This is so often the case with news photographers, for example. When they are doing what they call "garbage," they are wont to capture the moments of monumental tragedy, the ultrahuman tensions, but when they roll up their sleeves, clean their lenses, and pursue Art, they are likely to come up with pretty babies, small or large, or double exposures of dance teams.

In the case of François my fears were groundless. His painting is as straight and undissembling as is his drawing. His subject matter is casual—anything that happens to be nearby, from a coffee-pot to a cleaning woman; it may be bicycles standing around, or the butcher, the baker, bread, bottles, anything. Whatever object François paints immediately takes off on a life of its own, departing from anything even remotely ordinary.

André François

François carries a sketchbook with him much as a naturalist might carry a butterfly net. He has a sharp eye for the species in whose habitat he may happen to find himself. He constantly makes notes, and in these he seems to seek the ordinary, obvious features of people and places. For it is just in the intensification of ordinariness that he achieves the extraordinary.

Sometimes he lingers over one of his notebook sketches long enough to turn it into some intensely vital observation. I have one such brief sketch that he jotted down on a bitter winter's day. This is a glance at New York Harbor past the Statue of Liberty, the buildings hunched dark against steely white cold-looking water, the water whiter than the sky (a nice touch). This small item might be the harbor revisited by some person who had lived with it, hated it, loved it, and returned after some prolonged absence to have the view burst upon his sensibilities with powerful emotional

impact. That is the way the little sketch affects me; not so François. He had never seen the place before, unless perhaps from the deck of his incoming ship a few days earlier. Thus the power of quick reactions, a soft pencil, and a damp thumb!

Style is a curious thing with François. Style, real style in painting or drawing, is the natural modification of things seen through personal eyes, and those things drawn and painted by personal hands. It is the unified presentation of things, certainly, because when all of a man's work is truly personal it must be modified in the same way. That is what holds it together, rather than some deliberate attempt to achieve style by odd effects and mechanical devices. I have never seen a line-conscious line in François' work. I have never seen a splatter except one that might have occurred when the brush dropped or the paint or ink spilled. I have never seen an explosion used in his work to create effect; there are the natural explosions of ideas striking, those of haste, perhaps, but all this is organic and not sought after.

And while I cannot imagine anyone who would be quicker than he to shun pretentious affectation in the look of his work, I cannot, on the other hand, think of an artist whose work is more marked in its uniqueness of treatment. Line, as I have said, is with him the most direct route to saying something. His line is simple to the point of laughability. It probes, it searches for the thing it intends to depict. It sometimes strays off in the wrong direction, but it always seems to come home again without having lost its innocence. This quality is the essence of his humor as well as of his style. For even if the situations which François depicts were less amusing, if he never used a a caption, the line itself would provoke a laugh.

If man were a creature of dignity, there would be no place for François. But man, alas, is not a creature of dignity. When he is eating he is humped; when he is making love he is disheveled; when he pursues a beautiful woman he is shorter, nay, squatter than she. But she, ah, She! Delicately tiptoeing through life, the dream creature, the ever-tremulous, wearing a beatific smile on her big mouth, draping her choppy hair temptingly over her pillow; long at the waist, widely jutting at the hip, flat-footed, dumpy, shoulderless, François' woman is the essence of amiability and romantic love. Now she is Undine in a shabby hotel room, sitting appropriately in the washbasin; now she is man's perfect helpmeet, nearsightedly mending, while her large hand is poised domestically in midair. Now she walks in splendid medieval costume, her hat sitting over her eyes. But neither her sweetness nor her lust for love ever fails: however big her face, it always wears the most innocent and

TEXT CONTINUED ON PAGE 121

Autumn in France is the subject of this poster for the French Ministry of Tourism.

A creator of children's picture books who delights in sardonic representations of yawning alligators and stumbling plumed knights, François has also turned his talents to illustrating more adult diversions such as Honoré de Balzac's Rabelaisian tale about certain amatory and other pranks of fifteenth-century King Louis XI of France. At left, the earthy hero of *Les Aventures du Bon Roy Loys XI* stands in lugubrious posture overlooking the partners of his indecorous revels. François made these drawings for a German-language edition of Balzac's travesty of a medieval chronicle, published in Switzerland in 1957.

115

Far from spurning advertising art, François invests it with his own surprise attacks. Above, the woman devotedly mending a jockey's jacket is in fact promoting the French textile firm of Boussac, which used this image (greatly enlarged, and with real patches of cloth) in a trade exhibit. Left, the poster publicizing color film abroad departs radically from a stateside advertising tradition of happy vacationers amid canoes and barbecues in a state of Kodachrome Togetherness.

Commissioned to help sell a French pain-killing drug, Optalidon, François provided this ideograph of a clown under sedation airily mounting the beast that has just deprived him of a leg. Below, again concerned with the prevalence of monsters (and of men) François presents *Pongo the Monster* in a series of paintings on "Legends of the Sea" executed by various prominent artists as institutional advertisements in Great Britain for the Bunkering service of The Shell Petroleum Company, Ltd.

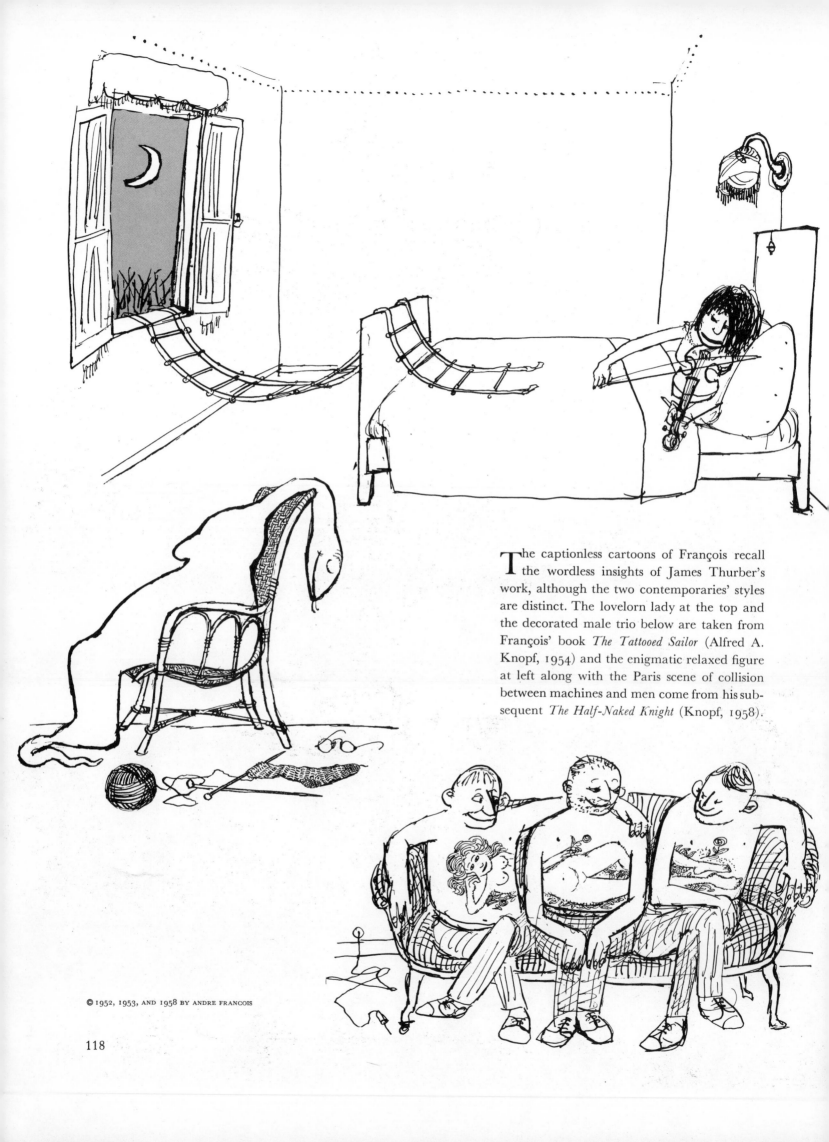

The captionless cartoons of François recall the wordless insights of James Thurber's work, although the two contemporaries' styles are distinct. The lovelorn lady at the top and the decorated male trio below are taken from François' book *The Tattooed Sailor* (Alfred A. Knopf, 1954) and the enigmatic relaxed figure at left along with the Paris scene of collision between machines and men come from his subsequent *The Half-Naked Knight* (Knopf, 1958).

119

the most expectant of smiles.

Thus humor and style are inseparable. But humor itself is not—never was—mere jocularity. Humor is a way of feeling about life, and when humor is great it is almost never without one of its opposite moods—tenderness, tragedy, concern for man's condition, recognition of man's frailties, sympathy with his idealism. Think of how closely the performances of Charlie Chaplin skirted the borders of sadness—which is, of course, the reason why he was always a *great* comedian, not just an entertainer. Humor was intrinsic in the style of Klee, the great stylist. Humor, bitter humor, was the informing spirit of James Ensor. It ran like a fire through the most powerful works of Goya, with their sardonic laughter at cruelty and injustice. Humor is present in the penetratingly realistic portraits of Velazquez, too, and in those of Eakins. Humor, that in-seeing kind of humor, accounts for the unrealistic style of Kokoschka; humor is present in every object and every painting that Picasso has ever made. Humor, then, one might say, is an eruption stemming straight out of keen understanding and often out of hurt idealism.

But these reasons are deep substrata and are slow to be recognized. Thus recently when François had an exhibition in Paris, it might have been predicted that the more serious critics would have little to say about his work. It was *l'art humoristique*, not a category for them. I am reminded of the story of how Guillaume Apollinaire sat for a portrait by Henri Rousseau—that was before Rousseau had been accepted as part of the art scene. The painting was exhibited at the Salon des Indépendents, and Apollinaire was so certain of what the critics would say about the work that he prewrote their comments and deposited them somewhere in affidavit form. His predictions were accurate. Rousseau was dismissed. But I can imagine what kind of press an exhibition of the works of this primitive master would enjoy today almost anywhere in the world.

François is deeply political; that is part of his seriousness. But when he makes political drawings they are, ironically enough, not good politics. They are good as humor, great as drawings, but are not sufficiently respectful of the political aims envisioned to constitute a real call to the colors. Politically effective drawings probably must not deviate from the clichés. If they do, they immediately cease, as the saying goes, "to communicate." François is incapable of

"Men Just Don't Understand" is the title of this recent François commentary on the human condition, in which a vacationer buries himself in a newspaper amid natural wonders and signs of romantic love.

producing a cliché. To him the clichés have only one kind of existence: as a part of man's clumsy, clambering life here on earth. As such, they come to life and are the stuff of his humor.

A great and impressive oil company once asked François to make a poster for them displaying their famous oil can in some conspicious but organic way. As I remember the poster, it was of two people lying in a bed, three corners of which were supported by bricks. The fourth corner was supported by the famous and familiar oil can. What more can one say about François and the cliché?

As for himself, he lives a quiet and circumspect life with his delightful wife, Margaret, and his children, Pierre and Katherine. Their house in Grisy-les-Plâtres is an old one, pleasantly modernized and always being added to. On our first visit there André explained to us that he and his family lived quite like Americans; and he exhibited his fine modern bathroom equipped with shower, toilet, bathtub, everything one could want in a bathroom, except pipes. For practical purposes there was a privy across the garden.

On our most recent visit we found the medieval stone house even more modernized. There were now two bathrooms complete with pipes. The second story of the house was greatly beautified, and the staircase leading to it swept grandly on upward to a third story—that is, in a fine diminishing perspective painted on a closet door.

Another improvement was an interesting wall of shelves that Margaret had asked for and needed in the living room. This useful addition was painstakingly painted on the wall and was laden with painted odds and ends of all sorts, complete with shadows and some accumulated dust and disorder. There was a dog—but I cannot recall whether the dog was painted or real.

The word "cartoon" has always seemed to me a peculiarly unsuitable one for such drawings as those of François and of the other artists whom I have mentioned here. A cartoon, as every informed reader knows, is the full-scale drawing through which a painter's mural designs are transferred to the wall. The present sense of the word was established sometime during the reign of Queen Victoria when the magazine *Punch* jestingly entered a competition for mural decorations for the houses of Parliament. Punch had always referred to its casual pictorial lampoonings as "pencilings," but it now adopted the word cartoon, which of course has become universal.

An older name for pictorial lampoons and broadsides was the "mad designe." This word belongs. It fits and ought to be revived. If anything describes the work of André François, it is "mad designe."

Ben Shahn, one of America's most eminent painters, is equally esteemed for his graphic work. Like his friend François, Shahn has contributed numerous illustrations to magazines and advertisements.

The Cave of Tiberius

CONTINUED FROM PAGE 107

tribuneship by his stepfather, Augustus. This office was one of the foundations of the imperial power. Suddenly Tiberius renounced the dignity and removed to Rhodes, saying that he did not wish to stand in the way of Augustus' true sons. But people believed that he was driven off by the perfidy of his wife, Julia, Augustus' daughter. He returned only after the Emperor had imprisoned her. Since Rhodes from the third century B.C. had been a principal center of Hellenistic culture, it is enticing for the detective-historian to speculate that the Emperor Tiberius—who could have arranged what he pleased—may have chosen to establish a gallery of the original Rhodian masterpieces which he had admired during his sojourn there.

The quantity of statuary unearthed at Sperlonga is enormous and the task by no means complete. A year after the work had begun more than 12,000 fragments had been found. About 6,000 had been numbered to aid in the process of reconstruction into their respective figures and groups.

The groups that could thus far be identified were Ganymedes seized by the eagle, Menelaus with the dead Patroclus, the theft of the Palladium, and a heretofore unknown version of Scylla devouring mariners. Besides these presumptive Hellenistic works were the huge leg and the hands and parts of the hair which might belong to a version of the Laocoön myth, as well as two splendid male torsos. The list to date concludes with the statue of a young girl, a charming portrait of a child, two Roman portrait heads, a child with a mask of Silenus, two dramatic masks of marble, and a marble votive disk with reliefs.

It is noteworthy that so many of these fragments from the grotto clearly belong to sculptural compositions of several figures. For sculptural groups in the round, composed of several forms in dynamic poses, were a particular accomplishment of the school of Rhodes. Another Rhodian hallmark was the masterful handling of drapery over figures disposed in violent action. The noblest example of this is the great winged Nike of Samothrace which is the glory of the Louvre. Epigraphy dates the Nike early in the second century B.C. This would be shortly before the execution of the reliefs for the great altar to Zeus at Pergamum which comprise the most celebrated and influential group of Hellenistic works that have survived. They are believed to have been created under the supervision of the Rhodian Menekratous. The reliefs portray a vast battle between gods and Giants and in them passion and violence are conveyed by the stunning handling of forms and drapery in motion, as well as by the awesome visages. The marble comes close to living, breathing life.

These characteristically Rhodian traits are recalled by one of the authentic treasures found in the grotto—the life-sized group representing Ganymedes being carried off by the eagle. Ganymedes was the son of King Tros, the Dardanian ruler who gave his name to Troy. Enamored of his surpassing beauty, Zeus desired him as his cupbearer on Mount Olympus. Some versions of the myth relate that Zeus himself took the form of an eagle and abducted the youth.

The Ganymedes subject is rare in sculpture, the only major marble being that in the Vatican Museum. Pliny, that copious recorder of sundry information, has described a version of Ganymedes' abduction which was created by Leochares, the Rhodian remembered as the decorator of the west façade of the Mausoleum at Halicarnassus, a Wonder of the ancient world. Wrote Pliny: "Leochares represented the eagle which feels what a treasure it is stealing in Ganymedes, and to whom it is bearing him, and using its talons gently, though the boy's garment protects him."

Since the subject is so unusual in the sculpture of antiquity which has survived, many assumed that the Vatican statue is the product of Leochares, whose epoch is established as some time around 366 B.C. by a citation in a letter of Plato's. The American scholar G. M. A. Richter, however, has pointed out that the Vatican statue is considerably later than this in date.

The Ganymedes of the grotto is clad in a short, clinging chiton which beautifully reveals the slightly striding body. This drapery appears close to that of the fluttering garments of the combatants of Pergamum, which were executed some time about 250 B.C. This Ganymedes is a serene figure, resigned to his fate. His body (executed in variegated Anatolian marble with the head of white marble) is gently held; the eagle caresses it, even as Pliny said. The proportions of the bird and the youth are more realistic than those of the Vatican group, and it has an air of less theatrical but more harmonious and subtle appeal. These features suggest that the Ganymedes of the grotto is earlier than the Vatican group but is likely closer to the date of the great Pergamum work than to Leochares' supposed date.

An exceptionally fine helmeted marble head was found early in the explorations at Sperlonga. The helmet shows reliefs of Heracles battling with a Centaur. Beneath it, the face is entirely destroyed. Nonetheless, the helmet so closely resembles that of the Menelaus in the Loggia dei Lanzi of Florence that Professor Jacopi and his associates kept searching for other fragments which might belong to the figures of Menelaus and Patroclus. They were rewarded by finding a rather oddly bent foot which corresponds to that of the Patroclus in Florence. Thereafter they were able to fit together other pieces which compose much of the mantle of Menelaus. And so the process continues.

The reconstruction of sculpture on such a scale as that in the grotto of Tiberius is like playing at a giant's jigsaw puzzle of 12,000 pieces, composed of as many puzzles within the puzzle as there are statues within the grotto. The Ganymedes group, although broken in several pieces, posed no great difficulty in restoration. The subject and its composition were clear enough. Likewise the helmet clue had suggested the presence of Menelaus with Patroclus and, though with painful slowness, that reconstruction proceeds.

Two other subjects, having self-evident "indicators" or iconographic clues, seem to be represented by the sculptural remains in the grotto of Tiberius. The first is a marble fragment of unusual interest: a male hand holding aloft the bust of a helmeted woman. That it is the *image* of a woman that the hand grasps is indicated by the much smaller scale of the female head. The configuration suggests that it is a representation of the theft of the Palladium, by Odysseus or Diomedes, during the Trojan War.

The Palladium was the wooden image of Pallas Athena which stood in the temple of the goddess within the citadel of Troy. Since it had been prophesied that Troy would fall only if the image were removed from the city, the cunning Odysseus, together with Diomedes, managed to steal it. The Romans chose not to believe this version of the myth, contending that the Palladium had not been stolen but saved after the sack of Troy and brought to Rome by Aeneas. Aeneas' voyage is, of course, commemorated in the *Aeneid* of Virgil. Thus it is possible that the sculpture in the cave represents the hand of Aeneas bearing the Palladium. But the workmanship seems more Greek than Roman in its finish. Curiously, Pallas Athena, if it is she, does not appear in the Periclean-style helmet but in a lower, closer-fitting headgear.

Professor Jacopi and his colleagues had reason to believe they would find one sculptural group incorporating the sea monster Scylla. Scylla had been changed from a beauty into a monster with six dogs' heads through the jealousy of Amphitrite or Circe. It was Scylla's fate and role to waylay mariners as they passed between her and her sister monster Charybdis. Legend locates both in the Strait of Messina. Representations of Scylla and her victims were already known to archaeologists from the study of gems, vases, and reliefs, but no statue was known. The presence of a "prototype" at Sperlonga was intimated by the finding of pieces of an inscription in Latin hexameters. It indicates that one Faustinus (a friend of Martial's who lived toward the end of the first century A.D.) had prepared a scenographic plan, or elaborate setting, within the grotto for the imperial family. The inscription alludes to a group

Tiberius

of statuary commemorating the cruel Scylla, and to the "straits" through which the ship of Odysseus passed.

Now this sign may have seemed clear enough for the archaeologists of Sperlonga to have gone lightheartedly about their work, expecting that sooner or later they would turn up the marble monster and her victims from Odysseus' bark. Not so simple; the grotto held a profusion of clues dismaying in their intricacies. Just outside its principal mouth, the archaeologists noticed a mass of rock carved into the shape of a ship's hull. They observed that it had once been covered with mosaics and had been finished off with a splendid marble prow, now shattered into splinters. Some of the mosaic work was reassembled to reveal the words NAVIS ARGO and beneath these a partially missing word with the letters PH. Nothing could be clearer than this. Here must be a gorgeous model of the ship *Argo*, on which Jason and his fellow Argonauts had voyaged in quest of the Golden Fleece. Several versions of the myth suggest that Jason, like Odysseus, had sailed past the ravenous Scylla. Which adventure with the monster was recorded by the sculpture of the grotto? In either case it would have been a capital idea in just such a place as this to make a grotesque monument to a sea monster that dwelt in a cavern. It is worth noting that to this day local legend associates a sea monster of some sort with the grotto.

Within the grotto lay further clues: a dog-like muzzle, parts of canine fangs embedded in a human leg, a curious fishy tail, part of a body gripped in a great paw, and some sections of serpent-like coils; the latter of which Professor Jacopi considered might belong to the Laocoön group. Also uncovered was the arresting head and torso of a bearded man whose expression was as one struck dumb with fear. These fragments would support the case for a heroic monument showing Scylla devouring the sailors of Odysseus. For Jason, who sailed under the protection of the goddess Hera, is not recorded to have lost any of his crew to Scylla.

Perhaps the most compelling argument for the presence of the Odysseus-Scylla group was the discovery of an extraordinarily fine head, probably that of Odysseus himself. It is the life-sized head of a bearded man, wearing the conical cap of the mariner, with which Odysseus is customarily shown. The cap is of one piece with the head of white marble, appearing to be a different color due to its roughly polished texture. The features are treated in the meticulously realistic manner of the best Hellenistic masters and the workmanship is superb. The bulging sinuses, bared teeth,

123

the gasping, breathing mouth instantly recall the handling of the visage of the Vatican's Laocoön and the passionate glances of the Giants of Pergamum.

As for the simultaneous presence of a replica of Jason's ship, the *Argo*, perhaps there was some arrangement in the grotto whereby the monster Scylla appeared to threaten the ships of both Odysseus and the other adventurer. Whether this is the case or not, the discovery of the first sculptural prototype of the Scylla myth is notable. Professor Jacopi has hypothesized that the similarity of the subject matter between Scylla and Laocoön—that is, men struggling with serpents or sea monsters—could mean that the Scylla group was the work of the three Rhodians, Hagesandros, Athenodoros, and Polydoros, who treated it as a variation of the Laocoön composition. Perhaps the inscription with their names is meant as a signature to the Scylla group. Definitive pronouncement must await the collection and restoration of all fragments that can be located.

The Ganymedes statue, the Navis Argo, the presumed head of Odysseus, and the Scylla remains are archaeological treasures; the more so because of their existence in the grotto of Tiberius. Yet the question that tantalizes specialists and amateurs alike is whether it is the original Laocoön or a later version of the subject which once stood in the cave, or, indeed, whether the heroic leg disinterred belonged to a Laocoön at all.

Studying the gigantic scale of the leg found in the grotto, with no apposite torso yet come to light, some archaeologists have theorized that the limb may have belonged to a statue of Polyphemus, the one-eyed Cyclops who imprisoned Odysseus and his comrades in his cave. Professor Jacopi believes that the smoothness of the modeled leg and its dynamic feeling belie this identification, although one unusual aspect of the leg is a finely carved tuft of hair over the instep of the foot, which is not present on the Vatican Laocoön.

Besides the leg, fragments of carefully worked hair remain along with two mighty hands—these in flexions which do not correspond to the Vatican's statue. Professor Jacopi has considered that the two beautiful, life-sized torsos unearthed in the cave might represent the dying sons of Laocoön caught in the serpents' toils, and has pointed out that the truncated left thigh of one of them is in a position similar to that of the boy at the left side of his father in the Vatican version. On the other hand, both these torsos appear to be those of mature men, while the figures that expired beside their father are depicted as youths in the Vatican group. Other observations also tend to detract from the Laocoön identification. Nowhere on the marble fragments yet found can be seen the body of a serpent crossing the leg of Laocoön, as occurs in the Vatican work. It is possible that the serpents were executed in separate pieces of marble and assembled with the male figures, but Pliny had made a point of the remarkable fact that the original Rhodian Laocoön was carved from a single block. This, however, is not the case with the Vatican statue for, as Michelangelo learned for himself, it had been joined from a number of pieces, contrary to Pliny's assertion.

Final assessment of the originality of the Sperlonga "Laocoön" must await further finds within the grotto or in the pools outside it, which have not yet been drained. It is possible that the missing parts that would resolve the question may be found, if they have not vanished from the earth centuries ago in the limekilns of the Christians.

Perhaps when all the works of art in this fantastic gallery are identified, it may be possible to discern a grand tableau, a total design, which is comprehensible when the figures that compose it are appreciated together rather than separately. The whole may have been just a gallery of Rhodian masterpieces collected by an emperor who had an affection for that island and an informed passion for its art. Still, there is the temptation to wonder if such a man would not have relished some symbolic scheme of which each selected statue were a part. Could all the figures portray heroes drawn from the *Iliad* and the *Odyssey?* The presence of Ganymedes denies this theory. But consider **Ganymedes**. He, too, was a Trojan; a Dardanian prince like Aeneas. And Aeneas, too, had sailed up to the Strait of Messina, where the dread Scylla lurked in her cavern lair. The Romans—who claimed descent from the semidivine Aeneas—held that Aeneas had borne the true Palladium to Rome, where it was guarded by the Vestal Virgins. Could it be that Tiberius had chosen to surround himself with monuments commemorating the glories claimed for the Trojan ancestors of imperial Rome? It is credible that there existed some such key to the sculptural embellishment of the grotto, although this notion may be farfetched.

Today Tiberius is nearly exonerated of the perverse reputation he has worn through the centuries. But the evidence of the grotto may show that Suetonius and Tacitus limned him truly. The Zeus-Ganymedes myth enjoyed wide popularity in Greece and Rome, for it was taken as justification for the unnatural love of a grown man for a youth. It is possible, after all, that Tiberius was the wretched Old Man of Capri whom his earliest biographers reviled, pleased to sanctify his grotto with the image of the comely youth who was loved and swept away by the great god Zeus.

These last are speculations. The shattered marbles strewn through the sea-laved cavern draw them out. For the observer, sitting by the shell of a German pillbox on the strand below Sperlonga, images of all that gaudy, imperial past crowd upon the consciousness. On these sands wars have ebbed and flowed like the Tyrrhenian Sea pounding ashore under the terra-cotta sun. Time loses its focus with the sound, and through the air, jiggling crazily in the heat, the figures of laborers appear to dance upon the terraces of the Emperor's villa. Behind them the black mouth of the grotto, still guarding its secrets, gapes with a grotesque mirth.

C. S. Lewis

TEXT CONTINUED FROM PAGE 67

Malacandra as Thulcandra the "Silent Planet." It lies behind an iron curtain.

In the harmonious Creation our planet stands, uniquely, as enemy-occupied territory. In Lewis's scheme a great angel of a certain category (Oyarsa, pl. Oyéresu) has in his charge each of the planets with all its beings. But the Oyarsa of Earth (Satan) alienated himself from God by the corruption of his own will, together with a host of angelic adherents; he and they stand exiled from deep heaven, confined within the orbit of our moon. He who was the shepherd of the planet has seduced his charges into rebellion and evil after his own kind, and his influence has led to their fall.

Here then is a twentieth-century variant of *Paradise Lost*, a new telling of the Christian myth of the fall of man. (To call it a myth does not mean that it is not true, it means that it states the truth in a symbolic story.) It dramatizes and clarifies for our age the Christian teaching about man's peculiar dilemma in the order of Creation. The tragic fact of man's condition is that he is other than he was intended to be; the deep springs of his will have been subverted—he cannot do consistently the good that he would do, but does instead the evil that he would not do. The Incarnation is seen as an action from without, a beachhead for the reconquest of the planet and the redemption of man. This action, in God's methods, is not an intervention by force but an invitation to free wills. Anyone may believe and accept the proffered redemption, but no one is compelled to accept it or to believe.

In contrast to our planet Lewis evokes the richly imagined, *un*fallen world of Malacandra, where several distinct orders of intelligent beings with souls live in harmony and obedience to their Creator ("whose service is perfect freedom").

Ransom is brought into the presence of the Oyarsa, or ruling angel, of Malacandra. From him Ransom learns the truth about the history and condition of his own planet. The machinations of Weston and Devine are frustrated and all are sent back to earth in the ship that had brought them, Ransom under special protection from the malice of his co-travelers.

In the next book Ransom, now voluntarily co-operating with the great angels in the service of God, is sent on a special mission to the planet Perelandra (Venus). Here is an analogue of the Garden of Eden story. Yet, as Lewis insists, it is different, for it is subsequent, and God does not do large things twice in the same way.

A new Eve is confronted with temptation. In this exotically beautiful world of rippling, floating islands on vast warm seas, the forbidden act is to stay overnight on the fixed lands before an appointed time has come.

There is a subtle tempter, embodied in the person of Professor Weston, who has come there as the voluntary servant of the corrupt Oyarsa of Earth but is later, as we shall see, wholly possessed by him. The newness of this Garden story is that *two* voices from the world that had known the tragedy of what Milton called "man's first disobedience" intervene in the decision which the woman of Perelandra must make. In short, where there had been one intervention (the serpent's) in Eve's fall, there is now a counterintervention to argue against the seduction.

In this story Lewis deepens our understanding of the nature of man's fall. We are given a poet's vision of what man was intended to be. The tempting of the first woman of Perelandra entails an extraordinarily intricate, far-reaching debate at the deepest level of moral theology.

Perelandra intensifies and extends all the qualities of *Out of the Silent Planet*. Intellectually it is much more exacting. Imaginatively and descriptively it is a more soaring flight, reaching its grand climax in a partial vision of the Great Dance, a kind of *Te Deum*, a praise of all the works of the Lord. It affirms that "All is gift." To any responsive reader it gives a unique experience, a purgation through exaltation and awe rather than the familiar Aristotelian one through pity and terror. It is the apex of the trilogy.

The third novel, *That Hideous Strength*, is a buoyant satire on the overweening pretensions of technology and the social sciences. Lewis had already gibed at the latter in *The Screwtape Letters*, in which the elder devil counsels the junior tempter:

Above all, do not attempt to use science (I mean, the real sciences) as a defence against Christianity. They will positively encourage him to think about realities he can't touch and see. There have been sad cases among the modern physicists. If he must dabble in science, keep him on economics and sociology.

In *That Hideous Strength* the forces of evil operate behind the front of a vast sociological institute with much money and political power: the N.I.C.E. (National Institute of Coordinated Experiments). Aspects of the N.I.C.E. are highly funny, but the picture grows grim as it reveals the intention, meaning, and motivation behind the boast that "this time we're going to get science applied to social problems and backed by the whole force of the state":

It does really look as if we now had the power to dig ourselves in as a species . . . to take control of our own destiny. If Science is really given a free hand; it can now take over the human race and re-condition it: make man a really efficient animal.

It pictures an attempt at the dehumanization of man fully as deadly as those imagined by Huxley and Orwell. This plan aims at "Man Immortal and Man Ubiquitous. . . . Man on the throne of the universe."

This vision, of course, is madness. The dream of man as supreme in Creation, with the ruthless totalitarianism that accompanies it, is inspired by the corrupt Oyarsa of Earth and his cohorts of banished angels. These are not known in their true nature to the men of the N.I.C.E., who would consider angels, good or bad, to be vulgar superstitions.

But against this dreadful threat of enslavement by a dehumanizing tyranny, a counterforce is poised of a kind imagined by neither Huxley nor Orwell in their famous novels of dark prophecy. The human protagonists guided by Ransom—who is now identified as the "Pendragon," the successor to King Arthur (in a mystical, not a political sense)—invoke the strength of Logres, the ancient Christian realm in the heart of England. Arthur's great magician, Merlin, is awakened from the magic sleep into which, in Malory's *Morte d'Arthur*, he had been cast. The great Oyéresu of the first two books lend their powers, through the voluntary vehicle of Merlin, so that the mighty coup prepared by the forces of the corrupted Oyarsa of Earth is thwarted.

In this sweeping theological fantasy, man is both reduced and exalted: reduced in the naked depiction of his self-wrought condition, exalted through the mystery of the Incarnation—that God became man for his salvation. In the trilogy, and also in an article called "Will We Lose God in Outer Space?" written for the *Christian Herald* in 1958, Lewis examines the question of man's uniqueness. What of other beings possessing both intelligence and souls who may be elsewhere in the universe, if not in our solar system?

On some planets the equivalents of man may be unfallen, still in the state God intended for them. If, elsewhere, there are other beings who have fallen, before or since man's fall, it is likely that God will have devised the appropriate means for their redemption, though not necessarily the same as the means for ours. That passionate skeptic, Mark Twain, far removed from Lewis's theology, had a similar idea in his story *Captain Stormfield's Visit to Heaven*. The Captain, entering Paradise by the wrong gate, is hard put to let the officials know from what obscure world he has come. "It's the one the Saviour saved," he says hopefully. The gateman bows his head at the Name, then says gently: "The worlds He has saved are like to the gates of heaven in number—none can count them."

Lewis, in his *Christian Herald* article, admonishes us against the interplanetary imperialism which Professor Weston attempts in *Out of the Silent Planet*. Against the creatures we might find on other worlds, he fears that

we shall, if we can, commit all the crimes we have already committed against creatures certainly human but differing from us in features and pigmentation. . . . Our loyalty is due not to our species but to God. Those who are, or can become, His sons, are our real brothers, even if they have shells or tusks. . . . It is spiritual not biological kinship that counts.

In the trilogy, Lewis focuses attention upon forms of the sin of pride: the desire to affirm man as God or as godlike, the ambition to dominate the universe, to supersede other species, to live forever.

In Prince Caspian, *the visitors and intruders from Earth leave Narnia by walking through a magic door.*

He lays the basis for his thesis in an ingenious presentation of the doctrine of sin—an unpopular word in the modern vocabulary. The beings of his unfallen world, Malacandra, have no word for sin or evil. They grope for the concept through the word "bent." This is a most revealing monosyllable.

We never use "bent" to describe the *first state* of anything; hence it tells us that there was a previous condition. It contains various possibilities, though not certainties, of a future condition: restored to the original state, remaining the same, or becoming more bent to the point of being broken. When an object is bent it will be misshapen or will malfunction or will fail to function at all. A bent arrow or a bent gun will miss the mark. Christianity does not know evil as a separate entity, but understands all evil as the corruption of an original good, susceptible of a possible redemption. It is this corruption which is sin. Its home base is in the will.

In the trilogy, Weston, the space-conquering physicist, displays the most dangerous form of bentness. It is the corruption of great gifts and above crude self-seeking. He would make man, and the seed of man, supreme. He declares to the Oyarsa of Malacandra:

Life is greater than any system of morality; her claims are absolute . . . I am prepared without flinching to plant the flag of man on the soil of Malacandra: to march on, step by step, superseding, where necessary, the lower forms of life that we find, claiming planet after planet, system after system, till our posterity—whatever strange form and yet unguessed mentality they have assumed—dwell in the universe wherever the universe is habitable.

Of Weston's ambition, Oyarsa asks:

Does he think he could go to the great worlds? Does he think Maleldil [God] wants a race to live for ever?

Modern man ignores, and Lewis reminds him of, that portion of Christian doctrine called eschatology, or Last Things. It shocked many and made headlines not long ago when the Archbishop of Canterbury said that God's purposes might contain the possibility of man destroying his species with the hydrogen bomb. But in Lewis's words, there is "now at last a real chance for fallen Man to shake off that limitation of his powers which mercy had imposed upon him as a protection from the full results of his fall."

In *Perelandra* Weston finally delivers himself wholly into the power of the lord of the silent planet, the "bent Oyarsa" (Satan), by the rash words "I call that Force into me completely." As he is rent by the paroxysms of demonic possession, the true Weston dies while his body remains an "unman," a walking, speaking shell, animated by the Power with whom Ransom must wage his portentous struggle in direct and deadly combat. Lewis's specific point here is that demonic possession in any degree, like redemption, is not a matter of imposed outside force, but a matter of invitation. God will not force Himself upon the soul who does not invite Him, and Satan cannot.

I rate high among Lewis's accomplishments a work generally less well known, as yet, than the trilogy, but for which I predict a growing reputation and a long life. This is the series of seven books for children which composes the Chronicles of Narnia, published between 1950 and 1956. Not in order of their original appearance, but in the strict order of their internal chronology, they are: *The Magician's Nephew; The Lion, the Witch, and the Wardrobe; The Horse and His Boy; Prince Caspian; The Voyage of the Dawn-Treader; The Silver Chair;* and *The Last Battle.*

As "space" is the medium of the trilogy, another common science-fiction element, "dimension," is that of the children's series. Narnia is a realm visited at different times by a number of Earth children. Time in Narnia and time on Earth are disparate, and Lewis is able to disclose to us within one earthly generation all the centuries of Narnian time from its creation to the fulfillment of Last Things, the end of the Narnian world (a joyous, not a sorrowful, culmination).

Dominating the stories is the glowing, golden figure of the Lion, Aslan. (The lion is an ancient but now little known Christ symbol in Christian art.) He is a real lion but he is also the Second Person of the Trinity, just as in the Nicene Creed Christ is "Very God of very God" who was made man. Aslan is the One "by whom all things were made" and by whom Narnian time is drawn to its close. Lewis shows us that act of creation, Narnia brought into existence and beauty through the song of Aslan; we see, too, the end-that-is-a-beginning as He changes all things, abolishes all evil, and calls His own to Him in new being. But nothing in the chronicles matches for audacity of conception and boldness of invention the analogue of the crucifixation and resurrection. Aslan surrenders Himself to cruel death as a substitute for others, in fulfillment of ancient law. He rises again to watch over His creation.

Narnia is peopled with bright, memorable figures: Reepicheep, the valiant mouse; Puddleglum, the marshwiggle; dwarfs, giants, satyrs, beavers, and a wealth of other beasts and creatures. The child who reads of Narnia, while having an enchanting adventure, will see human behavior in its full range; and he will learn the Christian concept of his nature and destiny as a creature.

Lewis is at the center of the great debate: What is the reality of our being and our environment? The doctrine of Creation (that all things were made by God) and the doctrine of man (as a free, responsible, guilty, redeemable creature of God) are high in his concern. This is the source of the vigor of his work, the cause of the extremes of acceptance and rejection which he arouses in people—for Lewis is bitterly attacked by those to whom his Christian premises are unsympathetic or unreal. Even within Christian circles he has his foes. Some are shocked by his imaginative freshness of statement and count him unorthodox. At another extreme he is regarded as too orthodox by those who will not accept the bold, relentless terms in which he sometimes dramatizes the alternatives between which man must choose.

His war is upon the diminishers of humanity. In one of his short polemics, *The Abolition of Man*, he traces and celebrates that great, world-embracing, humane, enlightened, and religious vision which is common to Platonic, Aristotelian, Stoic, Christian, and Oriental philosophy alike. For brevity he calls it by its Chinese name, the *Tao*. It is against the *Tao*, as much as any creed, that war is waged by those who deny the objective reality of what man calls beauty, truth, morality, honor, justice, love, and belief, demeaning the reality in which we live by claiming that these entities are mere subjective states of mind.

I am grateful to Lewis for some of my richest experiences of mind and heart. Thanks to him, I can remember with his hero, Ransom, "the Malacandrian sky at morning" and those splendid sights of its night sky, the Milky Way "rising like a constellation behind the mountain-tops—a dazzling necklace of lights brilliant as planets, slowly heaving itself up till it fills a fifth of the sky and now leaves a belt of blackness between itself and the horizon," and then, "the true king of night . . . Jupiter rising beyond the Asteroids."

I can remember with him the awesome glimpse of the Great Dance at the conclusion of *Perelandra*—that Great Dance which is the ultimate order and purpose of all created things.

Am I to say these are not real? I count them among the great symbolic visions of ultimate reality which reveal to us that we are more—and are a part of more—than the data of our senses can record.

Edmund Fuller is the author of a recent critical study, Man in Modern Fiction, *and of two novels. He was formerly on the faculty of Columbia University and now teaches at Kent School in Connecticut.*

Wedgwood and His Friends

CONTINUED FROM PAGE 96

Lucretia was discarded on the grounds of stupidity and Sabrina, despite her beauty and "more glowing bloom," lacked the necessary courage. Like all true disciples of Rousseau in the eighteenth century, Day was convinced of the value of ruggedness. To test poor Sabrina's courage and indifference to pain, he fired pistols close to her ear, blazed away at her petticoats, and dropped hot sealing wax down her neck. The results were unsatisfactory. Far from displaying the Spartan indifference he had hoped for, the tiresome child sobbed and screamed in fear. His faith in Rousseau somewhat shaken, Day sadly married her off as incorrigibly unsuitable. On other problems Day was no less eccentric, but his humanitarian and liberal principles were so blatantly honest and his writings so heartfelt that he was welcomed into the Lunar Society and Wedgwood's circle. He even managed to find an amenable and loving wife.

His closest friend, Richard Lovell Edgeworth, was outstanding in a more conventional manner. An excess of wives was his problem—he married four times and produced twenty-two children. With his landed estates in Ireland, he could afford to indulge himself and he never tired of doing so. As he wrote of himself:

> How I baffle human woes
> Woman, lovely woman knows.

Edgeworth, however, had a natural facility for friendship, as well as for courtship. His keen interest in mechanics and his inventive gifts, his literary abilities, and above all his spontaneous gaiety won him the esteem and affection of first Keir and Small and then the rest of this circle. His major projects were invariably ingenious and invariably failures. His mechanical wooden horse, his sailing carriage, and his huge hollow wheel in which by walking, like a mouse in a treadmill, a man could travel far faster than he could walk were typically extravagant ideas. When they did prove workable, it was usually in a hair-raising manner: the sailing carriage broke its moorings and threatened to disrupt the more conventional traffic before it was dramatically halted; and the walking wheel proved its speed by careering through Reading with a small boy inside it, only to smash itself to pieces in a chalk pit—happily discarding its passenger on the way. Undismayed by such setbacks, Edgeworth would transfer his interest elsewhere and by his enthusiasm captivate his friends into considering his latest scheme. Some of his more prosaic ideas were accepted: for his machine for cutting turnips he won the gold medal from the Society of Arts and for his perambulator, a silver medal. But he too, like Day and Darwin, was a bigger man than his achievements suggest, and he played an important part in the life of the group—his ideas acted like a scientific yeast and his presence like a social catalyst.

The core of this circle is completed by the two who had,

perhaps, the greatest worldly success—Boulton and Watt—and by the one who has been credited with the least, Wedgwood's partner, Thomas Bentley. The contrast between Boulton and Watt was marked. Boulton was the natural autocrat. Distinguished in looks and dignified in bearing, he immediately suggested the kingly. Yet unlike his silent partner he was amiable, confident, and outward going. As Watt wrote, his "active and sanguine disposition served to counterbalance the despondency and diffidence which were natural to me." As a team, however, they functioned superbly and Boulton deserves as much credit as Watt for the success of the steam engine. He risked his capital—and that of his friends—to make, market, promote, and distribute an invention which many men regarded as unsalable.

Bentley was completely different. His fame rests on personal charm, the most perishable of historical evidence and the most easily lost. His name now surfaces only occasionally in the pages of history and his usual haunt is in the footnotes. Lacking the distinguishing label of accomplishment, he has survived only as an adjunct to the great, but he was Wedgwood's closest friend and as such was an integral part of this Midland group.

Such were the diverse characters who made up the hard core of Wedgwood's circle of friends. Others equally fascinating collected on the fringe: Anna Seward, the Swan of Lichfield, seeking solace for unrequited love in her poetry and the company of the great, collected rare and interesting people with the avidity of a big game hunter and entertained her captures at Lichfield like an eighteenth-century Mme Verdurin; Joseph Priestley, the strange gifted scientist, his mercurial mind flitting from science to politics like an excited moth, who eventually had to flee to America from the fury of the Birmingham mob; James Keir, "a mighty chemist and a very agreeable man," who translated Macquer's *Dictionary of Chemistry;* and the kindly Dr. Small, who experimented in chemistry and, pandering to Day's taste for women with long petticoats and large white arms, scoured the Midlands to find him a suitable mate.

Devotion to science and a respect for the arts were not the only factors common to these people, for if it was this that cemented their friendship, there were other powerful ties of opinion. They shared a common attitude to society, to government, and to the nature of liberty.

They had decided and optimistic views on society. They saw men as improvable—even perfectible. They saw society as it was—crude, filthy, incompetent, and wasteful—and they wished to reform it. They read Bentham, Wilberforce, Howard, Cartwright, Malthus, and of course Priestley, and they believed what they read. They were not, however, idle theorists conjuring up utopias in a golden haze of false optimism. They had built their successes on humble beginnings and their lives were pockmarked with stories of endurance and application: Stubbs working unassisted on the anatomy of the horse at his lonely Lincolnshire farmhouse and stuffing the veins with wax to slow down the putrefaction of his models; Brindley struggling against diabetes for the last eight years of his life and giving advice even on his deathbed; and Wedgwood having his injured leg amputated to ease his movements through his works and the narrow streets of the potteries. Though practical men, they had suffered for their beliefs and they expected devotion of the same order from the rest of society.

The manufacturers wished to discipline their workmen for their own good. They were not to have the luxury of downing tools at the time of a wake or a fair, nor of working for three days in order to drink for four. In return they were offered security.

The instincts of Wedgwood's friends were undoubtedly humanitarian. Much of what the manufacturers amongst them did was for their own benefit, but there were other things clearly designed solely for the improvement of man's lot. Wedgwood built new houses for his workmen; Watt supported the Pneumatic Institution for the treatment of consumption. Darwin gave his services free of charge to the poor; Boulton built a home for orphans, parish apprentices, and hospital boys; and Sir Joseph Banks, another friend of Wedgwood's, preferred at considerable sacrifice to himself to wait until his tenants died rather than terminate their leases. Thomas Day, characteristically, carried his humanitarian principles even further. He let the birds feed from his crops undisturbed, left insects unmolested with almost Buddhist consistency, and defined life's enjoyment as "feeding the hungry, clothing the naked and . . . alleviating the distress of the most wretched and most miserable of mankind."

John Howard, friend of this circle, worked for prison reform, striding through the foul-smelling jails of eighteenth-century England, in Darwin's words, "if not to sever, to relax the chains." They themselves pressed for the abo-

A wine ticket for the Bastille Day dinner that set off the Birmingham riots of 1791.

lition of slavery. Wedgwood convinced Anna Seward of the necessity for it; Day wrote "The Dying Negro" and other poems; Wedgwood and Bentley produced their famous cameo medallion of the kneeling slave asking, "Am I not a man and a brother?"; and Darwin wrote to Wedgwood proposing an exhibition in the House of Commons of the "muzzles and gags made at Birmingham for the slaves in our islands" and of "one of their long whips or wire tails." He too expressed himself in verse on this "detestable traffic in human creatures." His description was clearly designed to accompany Wedgwood's medallion, for he wrote, with greater feeling than felicity:

> —The Slave, in chains, on supplicating knee
> Spreads his wide arms, and lifts his eyes to Thee;
> With hunger pale, with wounds and toil oppress'd,
> "Are we not Brethren?" Sorrow choaks the rest.

and he concluded with a warning to the apathetic:

HE WHO ALLOWS OPPRESSION SHARES THE CRIME.

Together they had a powerful effect and Benjamin Franklin wrote to Wedgwood from America to congratulate them on their efforts.

Closely allied to their philanthropy was the political liberalism of this group. Not that they acted as a body in politics, or even entirely agreed. The Lunar Society had its tory elements, just as it had its Christians and atheists. As Priestley wrote: "The members had nothing to do with the religious or political principles of each other, we were united by a common love of science, which we thought sufficient to bring together persons of all distinctions— Christians, Jews, Mohametans and Heathens, Monarchists and Republicans." But Day, Darwin, Keir, Small, Edgeworth, Wedgwood, and Bentley were convinced liberals, as of course was Priestley.

Their attitude to the American war was typical of their feelings. Like all intelligent men they found the folly of their own country the hardest to bear, and they denounced the actions of the ministry with the bitterness of the betrayed. As Wedgwood ironically put it: "I could as soon pardon [a man] making crockery ware malleable [as keeping] our present set of rulers" in power. Anna Seward dared to rebuke even the mighty Dr. Johnson for his anti-American opinions; Wedgwood and Bentley wrote in horror and alarm at the idiocy and incompetence of it all; and Thomas Day thundered his indignation in verse.

They were not satisfied with mere abuse, however. The folly of the American war did more than disturb their conscience; it insulted their sense of competence, underlined their feeling of frustration, and strengthened their desire for parliamentary reform. In defeat minor irritants seemed gross afflictions. What had seemed regrettable now seemed intolerable. Wedgwood and his friends were sickened by the corruption of Parliament, infuriated by the venality of local elections, and frustrated by their lack of power to reform them. Wedgwood might rejoice that America was free and greet the French Revolution as glorious, but it was little compensation for the situation in England. They had built roads, financed canals, conquered steam, and organized the factory system. Now they wanted to extend such rational and systematic reform elsewhere. Half measures could not satisfy them. When in April, 1785, Pitt's abortive scheme for parliamentary reform was announced, Day spoke for them all when he wrote in contempt:

> When faithless senates venally betray;
> When each degenerate noble is a slave;
> When Britain falls an unresisting prey;
> What part befits the generous and the brave?

This is more an expression of their frustration than of their eupeptic optimism. But the optimism was there. They saw in the events in France and America the pointers to the future, and they rejoiced in their success. Not everyone shared their confidence and they met determined opposition. There was widespread anger at the beliefs of the Lunatics, as they were called. And when some of them held a dinner in Birmingham on July 14, 1791, to commemorate the French Revolution, an angry mob rioted in protest. Withering packed his belongings in a wagon, covered them with hay, and made for the open country; Priestley bolted with his family, first to London and eventually to America. Boulton and Watt armed their employees at Soho, barricaded their doors, and prepared to defend their beliefs. Only Priestley need have worried—his house was burnt to the ground, and with it his instruments, his library, and his manuscripts.

Alone they might have succumbed to such pressure but in their meetings and in their correspondence they presented a united front. They shared their hopes, their fears, and their resentments, and like all minorities under pressure, clung ever more tightly together. For such a feeling breeds loyalty; when allied to material success it also breeds confidence. And it was in the Lunar Society and its Midland ramifications that Wedgwood and his friends found their support, their certainty, and their authority.

Such solidarity was reinforced by intermarriage. The Darwins and the Wedgwoods, for example, became almost inextricably intermixed. Robert Waring Darwin, son of Erasmus, married Susannah Wedgwood, daughter of Josiah; their son, the famous Charles Darwin, married his cousin Emma Wedgwood; and their daughter married the younger Josiah Wedgwood. In the nineteenth century the children of these marriages were to see the success of many of the aims of this strange and gifted circle.

In the 1790's, however, this great group was fast breaking up. The turn of the century saw the death of many. Day was killed by a fall from his horse in 1789 (with characteristic perversity he had refused to have it broken in); Wedgwood died at Etruria of creeping gangrene in 1795; Darwin died in mid-sentence, writing to Edgeworth, in 1802; Priestley died in exile in Northumberland, Pennsylvania, in 1804; Boulton lingered on to 1809 with a painful and incurable disease of the kidney; Watt survived to solitary old age and died in 1819; Edgeworth, Keir, and Anna Seward filled their last years with biographies of their well-known friends but by 1820 they too were dead. The death of the Lunar Society—the formal expression of their friendship—marked the end of this famous circle of friends: the vacant seats remained unfilled, and the meetings were no longer held.

How much they meant to each other is clear from the *cri de cœur* of the one who was deprived of their company. Priestley, the lonely, embittered exile, as distrusted in his new land as he had been persecuted in his old, missed them most of all. "There are few things I more regret . . ." he wrote in a formal dedication to his friends, "than the loss of your society. . . . From our cheerful meetings I never absented myself voluntarily, and from my pleasing recollection they will never be absent." How close was their friendship is clear from Edgeworth's tribute. He wrote of their "mutual intimacy [which] has never been broken but by death," and concluded: "They proved altogether such a society, as few men have had the good fortune to live with; such an assemblage of friends as fewer still have had the happiness to possess and keep through life."

Neil McKendrick is a Fellow and College Lecturer in History at Gonville and Caius College, Cambridge. He has written a number of articles on Wedgwood and is now working on a definitive biography.

The Grand Seraglio

CONTINUED FROM PAGE 63

Kiusem. Kiusem persuaded Murad not to liquidate his younger brother Ibrahim but to keep him instead in the Cage; so that when Murad died in 1640 Ibrahim succeeded him, and Kiusem continued as Queen Mother and the power behind the throne.

Ibrahim was a homicidal maniac. He had been in the Cage since babyhood and, ever since he had been old enough to realize that he was a younger brother, had lived in daily expectation of the mutes with bowstrings. Therefore, when the viziers came to proclaim him Sultan, the first thing he did was to pile all the furniture in front of the door. Once convinced, however, that he was not to be killed but enthroned, he indulged himself in all of his criminal and crazy whims. He built a kiosk and lined it with sable; he threw gold sequins to the goldfish in the palace lake; he festooned his beard with precious jewels. One day in a fit of pique with his harem, he had each of his three hundred concubines put into a sack with a stone at her feet and drowned in the Sea of Marmara. (The story goes that some years later a diver, looking for a submerged wreck, descended into the Marmara and came up almost at once babbling incoherently about three hundred sacks, held upright by weights at one end, nodding and bowing in the current.) Ibrahim made a bath attendant the General of the Janissaries and an itinerant Arab singer Lord Chamberlain. Even Evliya Effendi, Murad's Boon Companion and a staunch admirer of Sultans, was obliged to write that "he was . . . not very intelligent." After eight years of Ibrahim, a janissary revolution overthrew him and put him back in the Cage where the mutes with bowstrings paid him an overdue visit. A son of Ibrahim succeeded to the throne, and the new Queen Mother very sensibly had the old one strangled and turned over her power to a capable vizier.

In earlier days the royal heirs had gained some knowledge of their empire by fighting at the front or governing distant provinces. But after the middle of the seventeenth century they never left the Cage. One Sultan, who succeeded to the throne after fifty years there, was unable to speak; another, who had employed his thirty-nine years there in copying and illuminating Korans, begged to be allowed to get on with it. The princes received very little education and what they did receive was apt to come from doctored textbooks. Prince Abdul Aziz, at the beginning of the nineteenth century, studied textbooks in which the Turks had never suffered a military defeat and the French Revolution had never happened. The princes' company was limited to that of eunuchs and women chosen for their barrenness.

Modern Turks, who are extremely proud of their history since 1920, prefer to ignore the seamy history of the Sultans. Because of this, and also because they are new to the idea of tourism and really can't see why a foreigner would be interested in browsing around any damp old Turkish buildings, the Museum of the Grand Seraglio is not only provocative but provoking. Enough treasure is there—emerald-encrusted coffee cups, plumed fans with diamonds hanging like dew among the plumes, a pure gold throne—to give a hint of the old, vast splendor. There are the Sultans' portraits—grim Sultans, foxy Sultans, obese and mad-eyed Sultans; there are marble balustrades and tattered brocade draperies, and one or two of the fountains that once made the whole palace murmurous with playing water. But the buildings are badly lit, the gardens raggle-taggle, and the few signs and labels maddeningly uninformative. It is as though the old palace still resented intruders and would like to keep them cooling their heels, as visiting ambassadors were kept at the Gate of the Executioner.

In the old days, when the Sultan was ready to grant an audience to a waiting ambassador, a herald cried out cordially, "Let the dogs be fed!" The audience always took place on a day when the Divan (the imperial council) was meeting and the janissaries were to be paid, so that the ambassador, already unstrung by what he had seen in the executioner's quarters, would be overwhelmed by the splendor of the viziers, the bottomlessness of the imperial coffers, and the ferocious appearance of the janissaries. Each vizier arrived at the palace separately, making with his entourage a little parade of his own. The Divan was so numerous that it took from four until ten in the morning to get itself together—all, of course, in a profound hush.

The walls and ceiling of the Hall of the Divan glittered with gold and gems, and the floor was paved with gold, a decorative touch that never failed to stun Western visitors. The Sultan did not appear in this room, but there was (and still is) a latticed bay window high up in its wall which was known as the Eye of the Sultan. "The King's private awful window," it was called. No one in the room below could tell whether His Majesty were there or not.

Sitting on a velvet couch, the ambassador was served pilau, about fifty different and rather monotonous dishes involving mutton or poultry, baklava, and rose-water sherbet, which, if it were summer, was cooled with ice brought by camel caravan from the Asiatic Mount Olympus, two hundred miles to the south. If the Turks wanted to be especially cordial, a brazier filled with burning aloe wood was passed under the ambassador's chin so that he could have the pleasure of saturating his beard with its incense.

Meanwhile the presents brought by the ambassador from his sovereign were unpacked and paraded around the Court of the Divan for everyone to take stock of. The Venetians always made sure to tuck in, among the glass and cut velvet, some Parmesan cheeses, for cheese was not made in Turkey. Louis XV sent mirrors for the harem. Queen Elizabeth sent

Murad III an organ; and to his favorite, Safiyeh, a Venetian woman who had been captured by Turkish pirates, she sent a small picture of herself in a diamond frame, enough cloth of gold for ten dresses, a case of crystal bottles, and some musk. Safiyeh wrote in a thank-you note, "the singular love which we have conceived one toward the other is like to a garden of pleasant birds," and sent Elizabeth some bloomers.

After dining with the viziers, the ambassador and the ranking gentlemen of his party were bundled into robes of silver or gold brocade trimmed with sable, in order to make them presentable enough for the royal eye, and were at last ushered into the audience chamber. This room, called the Throne Room Without (there being a Throne Room Within), stands just inside the Third Gate, or Gate of Happiness. (Gates, since ancient times in the Orient, have been associated with government and the dispensing of justice, which is why the throne room was placed here and why the Ottoman capital city was known as the Sublime Porte, taking this name from that of the main gate of the Seraglio.) The Throne Room Without was even more glittering than the Hall of the Divan, with ropes of pearls dangling from the ceiling and jeweled throne coverings varying in splendor according to the importance of the ambassador being received. An ambassador of Charles II of England, who was probably considered worth a good show, found the Sultan sitting on cloth of gold sewn with diamonds, with his feet, in little white leather shoes soft-soled like a baby's, planted on a green satin rug that was thickly barnacled with gold, pearls, and turquoises. Two pashas led the ambassador forward, pushed his head down until it almost touched the ground, and permitted him to kiss the hem of the Grand Seigneur's brocade sleeve. In response to this His Majesty merely stared at the wall, as he never took any notice of a Christian. If he wished to communicate with him he would do so through a vizier, who would refer to the ambassador's sovereign as "my brother" in order to make clear the Sultan's exalted position among rulers. The audience concluded, the visitors were attended back to their embassy by a great many janissaries and whirling dervishes, all of whom required tips.

The Throne Room Without was as far into the Seraglio as any foreigner or any Turk who did not belong in the palace was supposed to go. Beyond lay the Grand Seigneur's private apartments; the harem; the privy gardens; the quarters of pages and eunuchs; a mosque containing a mantle, a tooth, and some of the beard of the Prophet; and the Sultan's private treasury. All of these regions were so sacrosanct that in 1600 a Venetian who peered at the walls through a spyglass from the other side of the Golden Horn was put to death at once. One of the few outsiders who got this far was an Englishman named Dallam who was sent by Queen Elizabeth to set up the organ she had given the Sultan. He managed to bribe a eunuch to let him peer through a grille into a courtyard full of harem girls. "At the

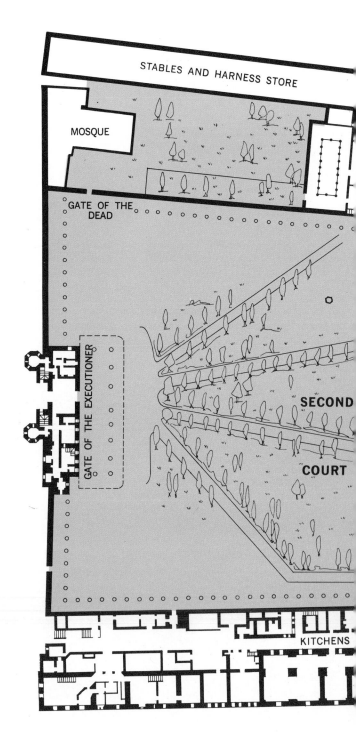

firste sighte of them I thoughte they had bene young men," he reports, "but when I saw the hare of their heades hange doone on their backes platted together with a tasle of smale pearle . . . and by other plaine tokens I did know them to be women, and verrie prettie ones in deede. Theie wore . . . a little capp . . . faire cheans of pearle . . . and juels in their ears; their coats weare like a souldier's mandilyon, som of red sattan and som of blew . . . britches of . . . fine clothe made of coton woll, as whyte as snow and as fine as lane. . . . Som of them did weare fine cordovan buskins, and some had their leges naked, with a goulde ringe on the smale of her

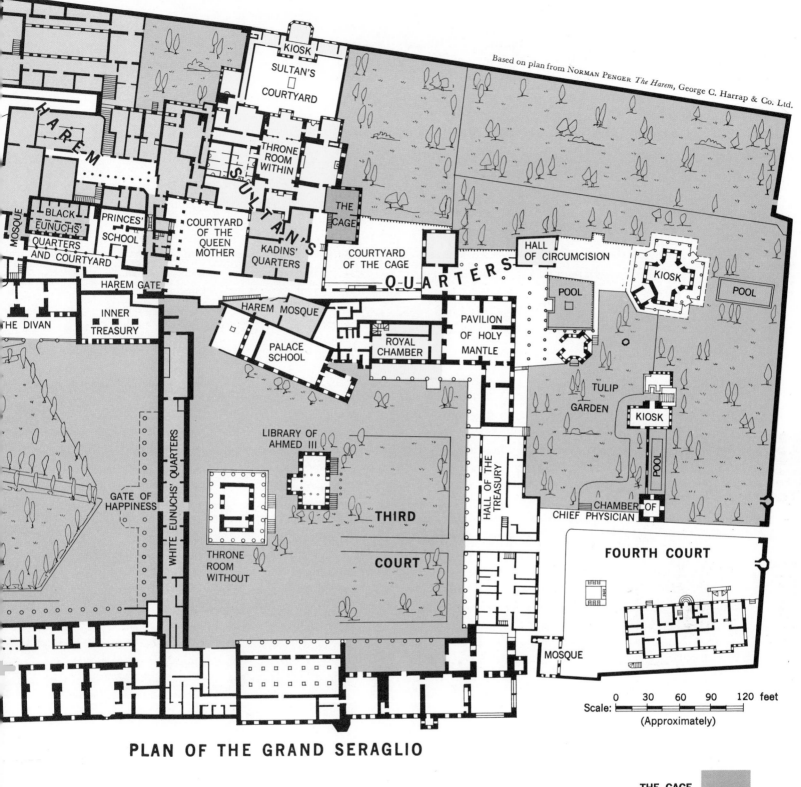

Based on plan from NORMAN PENGER *The Harem*, George C. Harrap & Co. Ltd.

PLAN OF THE GRAND SERAGLIO

THE CAGE

GARDENS

HAREM

SULTAN'S QUARTERS

EUNUCHS' QUARTERS

The Grand Seraglio, as this ground plan shows, had no architectural unity or over-all design. As a result of fires, continual rebuilding, and the accretions of four hundred years, it became a bewildering labyrinth of courtyards, chambers, and rooms of state. The First Court was not regarded as part of the palace proper. That began with the Gate of the Executioner (extreme left) which led to the Second Court. Diagonally across the court is the Divan. The first of its three square rooms was the glittering Hall of the Divan with its little latticed window, high up in the back wall, where the Sultan sat unseen by those below. Just inside the Gate of Happiness, in a separate pavilion, was the Throne Room Without—and that is as far as any foreigner, or almost any Turk, was allowed to go. In the forbidden territory above and beyond were the harem, the Sultan's private quarters, the Throne Room Within, and—grimmest of all Seraglio apartments—the Cage.

legg. I stood so longe looking upon them that he which had showed me all this kindnes began to be verrie angrie . . . and stamped his foote to make me give over looking; the which I was verrie lothe to dow, for that sighte did please me wondrous well."

The organ he set up was sixteen feet high and had a clock on top of it with a "holly bushe full of blacke birds and thrushis, which . . . did singe and shake their wynges." When Dallam demonstrated this to the Sultan, His Majesty asked an attendant "yf it would ever doo the lyke againe." The attendant answered that "it would doo the lyke again at the next houre." "I will see that," said the Grand Seigneur and sat down to wait. As the birds were adjusted to sing every fourth hour, Dallam, feeling dreadfully ill, had just sixty minutes to make intricate changes in the clockwork. He managed to get the birds in line and caught the next boat back to England.

Clocks were greatly prized in Turkey. They were not allowed to be made there or set up in public places for fear of lessening the importance and authority of the muezzins' five daily calls to prayer. Clockwork toys were coveted even more. Among Mohammed the Conqueror's favorite booty at the taking of Constantinople was a pair of golden lions that roared and a golden tree, big enough for a man to sit under, full of singing birds. A French merchant in 1685 was able to get a look inside the harem by bribing the Chief Black Eunuch with a mechanical man playing a drum.

The Turks acquired from the Byzantines not only mechanical toys but a good many habits now regarded as typically Turkish: the seclusion of women, the use of eunuchs as palace functionaries, the seclusion and semideification of the Royal Person, strict hierarchy and ceremony at court, and the luxury and fierce intrigue among powerful officials. The early Turkish rulers had been easily accessible to their people; but by the time of Suleiman the Magnificent, in the century after the conquest of Constantinople, the only remnant of the Sultan's ancient accessibility was in his riding out every Friday to the mosque of Aya Sofia (formerly the great church of Hagia Sophia). At this time any subject of the realm had the right to present a petition. He did so by writing down his grievance, tying the paper to the end of a long stick, and prostrating himself in the street. When the Sultan rode by on a horse whose mane was tied with diamond tassels, the petitioner, face to the ground, agitated the stick in the air and his petition was collected by an attendant.

When he got back to the palace dinner would be served, the monarch eating alone and in silence, as nobody was worthy to eat with him. Because of the ban on noise, mutes were his favorite companions. At table he was surrounded with them, and he conversed with them in sign language, threw them scraps from the table, kicked them, and tossed them gold pieces. He sat at a low revolving table resembling a Lazy Susan and covered with Bulgar leather. According to Ottaviano Bon, who was reporting secondhand but had his information from a Chief White Eunuch, he had a "very rich wrought towel cast before him upon his knees to save his clothes," as he ate with his fingers. "He useth no salt at his Table, neither hath he any *Antepaste;* but immediately falls aboard the flesh, and having well fed, closeth up his stomach with Bocklava, or some such like thing."

Serving the royal dinner required two hundred waiters. These arranged themselves in a long line, which extended through courtyards and corridors a hundred yards or so from the kitchen to the table. The dishes were passed from hand to hand, rapidly and without the smallest clatter. The royal service was always celadon, because this porcelain was supposed to have the property of rendering poisoned food harmless. Dropping a dish was punishable by death, not because of the value of the dish but because of the inexcusable racket, which may explain why the present-day museum has a vast collection of intact celadon.

After dinner the Grand Seigneur might go for a row in his 78-foot caïque. This was propelled at high speed by twenty-four specially assigned palace pages, who wore loose white garments and blue caps with red tassels. The Sultan sat in the stern under a gold-fringed crimson canopy, the only canopy allowed on the Bosporus. An eighteenth-century French ambassador who tried having one too received word from the Seraglio that diplomatic relations with France would be null and void until he got rid of it. Each foreign ambassador was allowed a ten-oar caïque and might fly his national flag, but he was not allowed to open an umbrella over his head. He might, if he wished, fan himself with a swan-feather fan.

Six caïques attended the large one bearing the Sultan. In the second was the Turban Bearer, who held up a turban and inclined it right and left to save the Sultan the effort of bowing. The oarsmen rowed standing, but the helmsman, who was also the Head Gardener and Chief Executioner and a very influential pasha, was allowed to sit in order to handle the rudder. Only he was permitted to converse with the Sultan as they skimmed along, and while they spoke, slaves rolled on the bottom of the boat and howled like dogs so that no one might hear what was being said.

The inner and residential part of the Seraglio was called the House of Happiness. It is hard to imagine who was happy there—certainly not the fifteen hundred women of the harem. For most of them life was like that in a strict boarding school from which there was never any graduation. Unless they were royal favorites they slept in dormitories accommodating ten or fifteen pallets on the floor, under the supervision of an old Moorish woman. Their education was limited to such matters as embroidery and dancing, the proper manner of bowing before the Sultan, or the playing of the *saz,* a long-necked, four-stringed affair that produced a plunking sound like a banjo. They could read the Koran and could write a little, although they had nobody to write to, having forever severed connection with their families. Each woman had one particular duty in the housekeeping arrangements: the First Mistress of the Coffee, for instance, took care of handing the Sultan his coffee when he visited the harem, and wore on her headdress a diamond pin in the shape of a coffeepot. They never went out of the palace except for occasional rides in a closed carriage or caïque. Any menservants who entered the harem—wood carriers, for example—walked between closed ranks of black eunuchs, and wore long woolen curls hanging down on each side of their faces to act as blinders. A doctor was sometimes allowed in the harem in case of serious illness, but he might examine only his patient's hand and pulse, the rest of her being smothered in quilts. If she was one of the Sultan's concubines, a silken veil covered her hand.

Many of these women lived and died without so much as a smile from His Majesty; others were smiled at, and for this reason promoted to the rank of *gözde*, meaning "in the eye" (of the Sultan) but never got any further than that; others were invited to the royal couch one or more times, which made them *ikbal*, or royal favorites, and entitled them to an increase in jewels and silk dresses and a private bedroom; and at the top of the ladder were the *kadins*, the first four concubines who produced children. The Sultan by tradition did not marry, but a *kadin* had the rank of wife except that no dower was settled on her, as is required in the Moslem marriage contract. The chief reason for this arrangement was to save money for the state, since a suitable dower for a Sultan's wife would have seriously embarrassed the treasury. Suleiman the Magnificent defied tradition and married his favorite, Roxelana; and it was she who moved the women's quarters—formerly in another part of the city—into the Seraglio. When Suleiman died, Roxelana became the power behind the throne of her son Selim the Sot, and for a hundred and fifty years thereafter a succession of ruthless, conniving queen mothers were the real rulers of Turkey. They were abetted by a verse in the Koran which reads, "Paradise is under the feet of thy Mother." Ottoman "momism" was particularly unattractive because these old ladies were not only dominating but as evil as could be. They had to be evil or they would have been trampled in the general rush of some fifteen hundred women for the most powerful position in the world.

In selecting a concubine, a Sultan held a regular weekly levee at which the virgins of the harem were brought in for his inspection; he dropped a handkerchief at the feet of the one who pleased him most, indicating that she was *gözde* and might hope for a summons to the royal bedchamber. When this came she was dressed in silk and jewels and perfumed with ambergris, with kohl on her eyes and henna on her fingernails, and conducted to the Sultan by the Chief Black Eunuch, all in strict secrecy so that the other women wouldn't be waiting to scratch her eyes out the moment she

got back. The Sultan's bed had wrought-silver bedposts topped with crystal lions holding in their teeth a gold cloth canopy. He liked the idea of owning a bed, like European rulers, but he slept, as his ancestors did in their tents, on a mattress spread on the floor. Two old Moorish women stood at his head with burning torches so that he might have light to say his beads at the last and the first hours of prayer, as the Koran frowns on praying in the dark. "Thus he rests," soliloquized Baudier, "which troubles all *Europe*, disquiets Asia and afflicts Africa."

A concubine arriving to spend the night was required to enter the bed from the foot, inching her way up under the covers until she lay level with the Sultan. This performance was also expected of husbands of the Sultan's daughters. These princesses, who wore a silver dagger at their belts to remind their consorts of who outranked whom, were in no demand at all as brides, for their husbands not only took orders from them, but could claim no special familiarity with their father-in-law. Children of such unions were not allowed at court at all, and the princesses' dowries could not be inherited by husband or children but reverted to the sultanate, as, indeed, did all the wealth of even the greatest pashas in this slave state.

The strange life of the Grand Seraglio began to languish after the destruction of the janissaries and the partial Europeanization of the Sultans. A new, elaborate palace was built on the Bosporus, and after 1851 the old Seraglio was used only to house the harems of Sultans who had died. One of the last official events there took place in 1909, after Abdul-Hamid II had been deposed and forcibly retired to Adrianople together with fifteen concubines, a guard of eunuchs, and his favorite cat. A public notice appeared in the newspapers, stating that anyone having a relative who was a member of the Imperial Harem might, by calling at the Seraglio, reclaim her. Telegrams bearing this news were sent to the headmen of villages in the Caucasus, since many of the women had come from there.

On an appointed day the entire harem, numbering nearly twelve hundred, was assembled without veils in a large hall, while hundreds of Caucasian mountaineers and other Christian people from outposts of the Turkish Empire filed through, seeking to recognize in these elegant ladies their daughters and sisters. Not all of the women were claimed or wanted to be. Some had been spoken for by rich pashas who were anxious for beautiful and delicately bred wives; some nobody came for; some quailed at the prospect of a peasant's life and chose to spend the rest of their days in reduced but genteel circumstances there in the old Seraglio, which thus ended as an old ladies' home.

Mary Cable began delving into the history of the Seraglio during a sojourn in Istanbul. She has worked on the editorial staffs of The New Yorker *and* Harper's Bazaar, *and now lives in Bremen, Germany.*

BARGAINING IN THE ARAB WORLD

The subtle ways in which people communicate by means other than words is the subject of a new book The Silent Language *by Edward T. Hall. An anthropologist, Dr. Hall was director of the State Department's Point Four Training Program and is now president of Overseas Training and Research, Inc., a concern that trains and advises American corporations with overseas interests. The following excerpt is reprinted by permission of the publisher, Doubleday & Company, Inc.*

Throughout the Middle East bargaining is an underlying pattern which is significantly different from the activity which goes under that name in our culture. Yet what is perceived on the surface (i.e., Arab methods of bargaining) looks familiar and is assumed to be the same. Nothing could be farther from the truth.

The American asks, "What percentage of the asking price shall I give as my first offer?" What he doesn't know is that there are several asking prices. Like the Eskimo who has many different words for snow, the Arab has many different asking prices, each with a different meaning. . . . The American pattern of bargaining is predicated on the assumption that each party has a high and a low point that is hidden (what he would like to get and what he will settle for). The function of the bargaining is to discover, if possible, what the opponent's points are without revealing one's own. The American in the Middle East, projecting his own unconscious pattern, will ask, "What percentage of the asking price do I give?" That is, "If he's asking ten pounds, will he settle for five?" This procedure is not only wrong but can end in trouble. The principle to be remembered is that instead of each party having a high and a low there is really only *one* principal point, which lies somewhere in the middle. Much like our latest stock market quotation, this point is determined, not by the two parties, but by the market or the situation. An important isolate in this pattern is that the price is never determined by the person or his wishes but always by some set of circumstances which are known to both parties. If they are not known it is assumed that they could be. Negotiation, therefore, swings around a central pivot. Ignorance of the position of the pivot opens one up to the worst type of exploitation, as well as loss of face. It doesn't matter whether it is a squash in the bazaar or a hydroelectric dam in the international market. The pattern remains constant. Above and below the central point there is a series of points which indicate what the two parties feel as they enter the field.

Here is how an Arab from Damascus described this process. The pivotal point was six piasters, the price of squash on the day he described. Above and below this there were four points. Any one of the top four might be the first price asked by the seller. Any one of the lower four represents the first offer made by the prospective buyer. The hidden or implicit meaning of this code is given opposite each step on the scale below. This meaning is not exact but represents a clue as to the attitudes of the two parties as they enter the bargaining process.

PIASTERS

12 or more . . . *complete ignorance on the part of the seller*		
10 . . . . *an insult, arguments and fights ensue, seller doesn't want to sell*	}	SELLER'S ASKING PRICES
8 . . . . *will sell, but let's continue bargaining*		
7 . . . . *will sell under the market*		
6 . . . . MARKET PRICE (THE PIVOT)		
5 . . . . *buyer really wants the squash, will pay over the market*		
4 . . . . *will buy*	}	BUYER'S OFFERING PRICES
2 . . . . *arguments and fighting, buyer doesn't want to buy*		
1 . . . . *ignorance of the value of the item on the part of the buyer*		

Considering the difference of meaning which is carried by a variation of one piaster, the question, "What percentage of the asking price do I give?" seems meaningless. Which asking price? The let's-do-business one, the let's-not-do-business one, or the let's-fight asking price? Other variations on this pattern have as many as five or six points above and below the line, each with its own meaning.

One cannot underestimate the importance of such patterns and the hold they have on people at all levels. In discussing our stand in Egypt during and directly following the Aswan Dam fiasco and before our position in the Middle East had deteriorated so badly, an Arab sympathetic to our cause expressed it this way. "If you don't give a little in bargaining, the other fellow will back up. If he gives two steps, you have to give two steps. If you don't, he will back up four." We didn't give our two steps and Nasser backed up four.